Psalm 115:16

The heaven, even the heavens, are the Lord's;
But the earth He has given to the children of men.

EXPLORING SECRETS
OF THE
HEAVENLY REALMS

BRUCE HINES

Exploring Secrets of the Heavenly Realms
The Mystery of Territorial Spirits

Special discounts are available on quantity purchases by corporations, associations, and other. Orders by US trade bookstores and wholesales-for details, contact the author via the website above.

First Edition, 2019
ISBN: 978-1-970062-06-9

Publisher: Kingdom Mysteries Publishing
817 W Park Row, Arlington, TX 76013

Printed in the United States of America

CONTENTS

FOREWORD

After watching Bruce write his first book in about 3 months, I was initially surprised at how quickly it all came about. Although, as I read through the book, I can personally remember the time frame of each story and each experience. I remember his first encounters with the fallen, when God would send them down to be judged, because we encountered them together. I was there when he received a prophecy from one of our National prophets about how God was going to make known to Bruce the structure of the kingdom of darkness. Because of the vast knowledge that God planned to share with Bruce, I watched and continue to watch, as the Lord drives Bruce to understand each spiritual experience through study, research and cause him to seek out counsel by contacting every person he could find who had true understanding about the fallen. Those specifically who had actually encountered them and who knew of them in the scriptures. I've watched his integrity as he studied to show himself approved before teaching the members of our church and ministry about the fallen. It was 7 years after his first encounter before he spoke publicly about the fallen. This book wasn't written in 3 months, it took over 20 years of combined study and the fruits of experience through healing and deliverance ministry.

Over the years we have prayed for thousands of people suffering from spiritual and emotional wounds, mental issues, as well as demonic complications all the while rejoicing with them in their healing. As we began to understand the structure of the fallen we began to rejoice with families as they were being reconciled and healed after the fallen were judged over the family lines.

If everyone would read and understand Exploring Secrets of the Heavenly Realms, churches, the people in them and their families, our cities, our nations and even our world would change. In Acts 28:27 Luke reminds us of what the prophet Isaiah said in Isaiah 6:9, 10. I pray that you will have the heart to understand, the ears to hear, the eyes to know and be acquainted with the mysteries of the heavenly realms. As you read the rest of this book, you will understand the difference between demons and the fallen.

Leah Ann Hines

Co-Founder and Pastor
Church in One Accord
www.churchinoneaccord.org

INTRODUCTION

We as Christians are involved in a wrestling match, both individually and corporately. The believer must understand the vast magnitude that surrounds spiritual warfare. To be victorious, we must understand the origin of this conflict and the structure of the kingdom of darkness. Yet the body of Christ has not made spiritual warfare or second heaven fallen angel warfare a prominent issue. The subject of territorial spirits or fallen angels has produced many books, articles, theologies, and bible scholars weighing in on the topic. But none of these investigations into territorial spirits or fallen angels has put in print what I describe in this book series. What authors agree on is the battle for the evangelization of the world is spiritual, involving spiritual warfare with high-ranking thrones, dominions, principalities, and powers who call themselves fallen angels or angelic majesties. So let us look at a scripture that will continually be looked upon throughout this book series:

> *For our struggle is not against flesh and blood, but against the rulers, against the powers, against the world forces of this darkness, against the spiritual forces of wickedness in the heavenly places. (NASB 1977)*

For our wrestling match is not against flesh and blood [contending only with physical opponents], not against persons with bodies, but against cosmic powers or fallen angels within four levels of the celestial realm who rule in various areas and descending orders of authority. Against world dominators of this present evil age, and against spiritual forces of wickedness in the heavenlies who are orderly tiered.

Here is my explanation of my expanded version of the cosmic hierarchy: This pictures a very highly structured organization of levels and grades according to numbers within a hierarchy who are well organized as a kingdom of four different dimensions in the second heaven. These different kinds of fallen angels within each of the four dimension have descending orders of authorities and different rulers and sub rulers according to grade and number responsible for different areas of authority in the second heaven which rule over the earth through the minds of mankind.

Derek Prince in his book "War in Heaven: Taking Your Place in the Epic Battle with Evil defines Ephesians 6:12 as, "For our wrestling match is not against flesh and blood, persons with bodies, but rulerships, against authorities, against the world dominators of this present darkness, against spiritual hosts or forces of wickedness in the heavenly places."

There are not many Christians who are wrestling. I could even say, there are very, very few Christians who are wrestling at all. Wrestling is the most intense form of conflict between two persons. Wrestling is total combat and that is the word Paul uses here. We are involved in total combat with spiritual forces who are without bodies in the terrestrial realm and fallen angels in celestial realm. As we look at the beginning God created the heavens and the earth, the heavens are plural, and the earth is singular. There is more than one heaven, this is stated very clearly in 2 Corinthians 12:1-4. Paul writes that he or someone he knows was caught up to the third heaven. If there is a third heaven, then there must be a first and a second. So we will be reading about the second heaven and the activity therein. This cosmic battle will rage on until all things have been placed under Christ Jesus feet.

In Isaiah 14:12, we read how Satan has fallen, and so the name of the evil angels who rebelled with Satan, the fallen ones. We also see that Satan has a throne, and his desire was to be above all of the other stars of God, or angels of God. This points to the different levels and creative orders of angels. We also read that there are different levels in heaven by his desire to raise his throne to the utmost heights of the sacred mountain. This shows us the multi-levels in the heavens.

We will also understand that when God created the heavens He did so in orders and with different powers. In so doing, God also assigned angelic armies of all ranks within each of the heavens and the multi-dimensions of those heavens. I have got your interest yet?

This book series is about scriptural evidence through power encounters with fallen angels and the coming war of the Church. Jesus left His disciples to carry on the war. The Church would have the same continual struggle against the devil, fallen angels, and demons as Jesus did. As expected, Jesus had prepared His disciples for fighting and winning the war to which He had assigned them. This book series is to open the eyes of the Church to the coming war with fallen angels, even though behind the scenes it is going on today! What I mean is face to face encounters of combat. The Church has been instructed by Christ to engage the kingdom of darkness on all levels, including fallen angel spiritual warfare and exhibit the manifold wisdom of God to the fallen powers of darkness.

It is my hope that this book series will touch generations and help them in spiritual warfare and the outpouring of Holy Spirit for the harvest of souls.

Bruce Hines

Author and Sr. Pastor
Church in One Accord

CHAPTER ONE

DETHRONING POWERS OF DARKNESS

I t is my hearts desire to bring into focus how the powers of darkness rule over regions within every nation. There have been 3 power ministries that have changed my life, Derek Prince, Bob Larson, and Benny Hinn. Since the day I read Benny Hinn's book "The Anointing," and touched powerfully in February 97, I have had a driving passion to see people touched and healed in Jesus' name through the person of the Holy Spirit. On Halloween night in 1998, I went to see a deliverance minister named Bob Larson. This was the first time I had ever seen demons obeying a minister. At the end of his service, I went to his prayer line, and I felt this amazing hot oil come on me as he anointed me. My eyes instantly popped open so I could see all those who had demons. It has been an awesome experience since, bringing deliverance to thousands who really want to be free. With these two power and authority anointing's, the Holy Spirit directed me to Derek Prince Ministries, where this powerful bible teacher helped cement my foundation on healing and deliverance. I have found over the years that the Holy Spirit's will for my life has been to show me the secrets of the kingdom of darkness, and to bring powerful breakthrough's to those who need healing. The key to the operation of the healing and deliverance anointing is twofold. The first key is the presence and power of the Holy Spirit. The second key is being fully trained, understanding scripturally how to dismantle the kingdom of darkness and also how God heals. In this book I will disclose those secrets. If we know how to handle each realm, healing and deliverance, then the only thing left is meeting the conditions that release the power of the living God.

I have read many books who promise breakthrough over regions through prayer, God's courtroom, healing or evangelism, and even though those are keys, the main breakthrough comes when deliverance takes place. Once a soul has experienced salvation, the forgiveness of sins confessed, and redeemed through Jesus' blood, and water baptized, the next step is to get those individuals delivered of evil spirits so they can receive the baptism of the Holy Spirit.

It is God's will and desire we undergo deliverance from the power of darkness in our soul and body. This comes through sanctification. Let me say it this way, the promise of the power of the age to come. Complete sanctification for every believer is in the age to come.

Salvation covers the spirit man. Jesus telling Nicodemus the principles of salvation. Jesus reveals, the flesh will always be influence by sin, because it is born of the flesh or the sinful nature. We inherited it through generation to generation. For an understanding of man's two natures, get my book entitled "The Mysteries Key to the New Testament". Jesus helps to clear Nicodemus' reasoning by saying that Spirit gives birth to spirit. Here is my point, as long as sin is in a region, there is no dominion or apostolic rule. There however is a coexistence or what I call the right to operate without opposition.

Just as Israel crossed into the promised land and moved forward to occupy, God gave the victory. The way to dethrone fallen angels over cities is to occupy and advance. To go out into the streets and win souls through the gospel of the Kingdom. This is both an individual revelation and a territorial unveiling. It is also Jesus' last order! If you have ever been in the military, then you know soldiers carry out their last order until receiving new ones.

We cannot deny that situations influence our flesh, disclosing to us that we are not free from this age and the influence of sin. When we drive around our cities, we see the influence of this evil age, sin. So I found the simple answer to dominion within a city is the personal salvation of someone. Jesus tells us in Matthew 9:38 (NASB), "Therefore beseech the Lord of the harvest to send out workers into His harvest." We are to pray that God would grant us favor as we go out into our cities with God's grace of salvation to those who believe. As we go out into our cities

With the gift of salvation, we are to heal the sick and cast out demons (Mat.10:7,8). This is exercising or enforcing the dominion of God's reign through Christ Jesus. The power and ministry of the Holy Spirit is the deposit given to those who believe, the power of the age to come.

We know from scripture that there are spiritual evil entities that have places of influence over individuals, cities, regions, and territories that determines atmospheres, culture, and daily living that reveals the natural. Most of mankind refuse to believe behind certain establishments, businesses, democracy's, and socialist governments are angelic hosts (armies), good or bad. Paul says, through individuals, up to and including governments. Ephesians 6:12 says, we are not warring against people, but the spiritual forces behind them. Through power evangelism, prayer, and establishing Holy Spirit power Churches, we subdue these wicked powers, so that the hearts and minds of mankind become set free and transferred out of the kingdom of darkness, into the Kingdom of Light. This is the main teaching of the book of Acts.

What Is Seen Reveals Who's In Control

The Bible shows us in scripture that what is unseen, the spirit realm, both good and bad, determines the control within individuals, cities, and jurisdiction. We see this every day, yet we become numb to our surroundings. We become desensitized through familiarity, and places of sin that give little thought to the destruction they bring. What has happened is evil supernatural forces, fallen angels with different levels of jurisdiction, and demons who have different powers, have legal rights through sin to oppress regions, and to keep mankind from the gospel of the Lord Jesus Christ? By suppressing the gospel, sin abounds. When the gospel of the Kingdom is not preached, sin abounds. These legal rights through sin are really curses that influence the minds of mankind. The regional curses are because of generation after generation continuing in the sins and iniquities of their forefathers. I see this both in non-believers and believing households, Churches, businesses, city government, through all their actions. Through noticeable behavior we see the reality of the unseen!

In Deuteronomy 28:23-24 (AMP), "The heaven which is over your head shall be bronze [giving no rain and blocking all prayers], and the earth which is under you, iron [hard to plow and yielding no produce]. The Lord will make the rain of your land powder and dust; from heaven it will come down on you until you are destroyed."

I love this scripture in the blessing and cursing chapter. It tells us what exactly we must do. When there is little to no breakthrough, the prayer of repentance, a movement of holiness, the prayer for an outpouring of God's Spirit, and power evangelism must take place. When a ministry sent to a dry and dusty region, persistence until the heavens begin to open is vital. One by one, God's people humble themselves and pray. The people of God overcome the fears of evangelism, and take their gifting's to the lost souls, this will bring glory to God. Sin hardens the atmosphere, yet ministers are not willing to call the Church to holiness. Prayer, holiness, and power evangelism softens the atmosphere and brings the rain. So how do we dethrone fallen angels in the second heaven, and the demonic powers that work for them? We become trained to win the lost. Go to God's courtroom and ask for our city. Prayers of repentance continually. Learn how to do spiritual warfare in the Celestial and Terrestrial realms. Power evangelism and preaching the Kingdom.

The book of Ephesians divulges that the Church is an army. Soldiers make up an army of many specialities, with many assignments. The body of Christ has many gifts, calling each member to do its part. Paul tells us that we must commit this army of soldiers to fight a war that is first global, continental, national, state, regional or county, city, and individual. In fact, this war is beyond global, it includes the second heaven or heavenly realms in all four of their dimensions, with their sub-dimensions or nine realms within each dimension. This is how I understand it today! The adjective that correctly explains this conflict is the word, universal.

FREEING OF THE MIND

In Isaiah 64:1-2, there is an intense combat situation going on within the different levels and sub-levels of the four dimensions of the heavenly realms. What is not said, but definition hints to, and combat encounters reveal, is such pressure put on the evil realms, both in the earth and in the heavens, through the Church, that it would cause the heavens to burst, to tear in a violent manner. Such pressure that the heavens would tear into pieces. This is what is defined as an open heaven. It is God's plan, as Jesus separated the heavens through fulfilling the Father's will, unveiling power ministry as the model, so now the Holy Spirit empowered Church must also do. God wants to shake the nations, but He will do most of it through His Church. It is the assignment of the Church to tear into pieces the heavenly realms, and the fallen angels who oppose us. We know if it was up to God, heaven and earth would be in direct contact all the time.

When the Church starts to cast out demonic spirits, eventually the fallen angels must come down and defend their territory. This has happened so many times in deliverance, both individually and over cities. As they come down, the more intense the prayer meetings become. Even mass deliverance takes on a new face. Instead of groups of demons being expelled, the fallen angels rule over his many groups of demons is removed and expelled. In this process the fallen angels then give over the minds of the believers to Christ Jesus (the freeing of the mind to renew) and comes out or pulls out of the mind.

When this happens, most say it feels like a painful extraction, or a pulling off the mind a veil or a covering, a lifting within that part of the mind or a dizziness that leaves. People often say that it feels like a vacuum, and when the fallen leave, all the demons come out at once. Most cough or vomit as the demons come out. Again, when fallen angels are leaving, in the mind of that person it feels like a pulling out, the painful drawing out of the mind, this is the freeing of the mind. The bible calls this the rending of the second heaven, the freeing of the human mind.

> *"And do not be conformed to this world, but be transformed by the renewing of your mind, that you may prove what the will of God is, that which is good and acceptable and perfect." Romans 12:2 NASB*

Conform to this world means to form or mold one's behavior in accordance with a particular pattern or set of standards. So we see the power of the mind, forming the way in which one acts. Paul says the mind of this evil age is the system of practices and standards associated with secular society (that is, without reference to any demands or requirements of God)—world system, world standards, world beliefs. The word for world in the Greek means "Age." We know this age is evil, ruled by the prince of the power of the air. Satan is not only a person but a metaphor for all the fallen angels who abandon their God given positions of authority. Each person is to undergo a renewing of the mind, that is to be free of the mind controlled by the fallen angels. Every believer will undergo two realms of deliverance, the mind and the body.

The deliverance of the mind is to cause something to become new and different, with the implication of becoming superior. The fall of mankind caused us to take on the nature and mindset of the fallen angels, producing in us evil deeds. But the mind freed by the power of the Holy Spirit becomes superior as it is renewed by the Word of God, and the power of God. The deliverance of the body is to expel demons, but the deliverance of the mind is to have the fallen angels pull out through judgment.

The evil mindset or will of humanity, controlled by fallen angels, first divides humanity from the Word of God. Second, it wants us to reason away God's truth. And third, it wants our thoughts to reject God's truth and ways. The mind of the believer is to undergo and experience an examination, tearing down false knowledge, beliefs, and actions. Experiencing through the Word of God and the Holy Spirit, a superior mindset with new hearts and new ways of understanding. This is the mind of Christ. The major shift in the mind of a believer comes when the fallen angels come out of or removed from the mind, and the mind is no longer blinded. People tell me that their understanding of the Word of God becomes clearer and God's thoughts or flow become more intense. Why? We lifted or removed the veil!

James chapter one tells us we first become hearers of the Word and then become doers of the Word. This is the mind freed from the fallen angels. James says, it is not the man who hears the Word, but the doer, this is the freed mind. But the fallen angels cause most not to hear it, but resist those who desire the doing. James says the Word of God is like a mirror, an examination of our minds. Yet, this is what the fallen angels war against. Trying to blind the minds of man. As mankind looks into that mirror, the evil fallen angels guard the mindset of believers and non-believers, so that no one understands and becomes a doer and experiencing the law of liberty.

> *"Therefore, gird your minds for action, keep sober in spirit, fix your hope completely on the grace to be brought to you at the revelation of Jesus Christ. As obedient children, do not be conformed to the former lust which were yours in your ignorance." 1 Peter 1:14*

Derek Prince would say about the word therefore, to find out what it is there for. Peter is challenging the believers of this great salvation and the glories they have, even God's holy angels long to look into. The mind freed from the fallen is one who's mind is ready for action. Someone ready to roll up their sleeves and go to work. This believer girds or tucks in the robe into the belt of truth and is now ready to run the race set before them.

The believer is ready to monitor and restrain the work of fallen angels and demonic spirits that influence and control mankind's mind through acts of evil. We must set our hope on the power of the age to come. How does that happen? By experiencing that power now, in this evil age. This happens as we live under a different mindset. We are obedient and responsive to the Holy Spirit and the Word of God. The mind that reasons over scripture, is the mind held captive by the fallen angels. Notice Peter states that those who are conformed to the lusts of this age, are controlled in their minds by the fallen angels and it is revealed by evil acts.

> *"And you were dead in your trespasses and sins, in which you formerly walked according to the course of this world, according to the prince of the power of the air, of the spirit that is now working in the sons of disobedience. Among them we too all formerly lived in the lusts of our flesh, indulging the desires of the flesh and of the mind, and were by nature children of wrath, even as the rest." Ephesians 2:1-3*

This is what the fallen angels, who are the fathers of demons did; overstepping the boundaries God had given them. We too sin when mankind acts or oversteps laws or boundaries in which God has ordained mankind to live by. Paul is saying, formerly we lived and behaved under the control of a throne, a prince, a supernatural force and power. Notice the definition is plural, but also referring to Satan. Paul says Satan has a throne, and there are many fallen angels who also have thrones under his control and command. They are supernatural powers having different and singular assignments and roles in controlling the destiny and activities of human beings. Since the definition is plural, and it refers to supernatural forces and powers, it means many thrones within each of the four dimensions of the second heaven. We will talk more about this in the next chapter!

So in dethroning the second heaven over cities, there are multiple layers of thrones and sub-thrones we must pull down and judge according to scripture. We find this in Psalm 82, and I have seen this happen at least a thousand times. To remove evil angels over cities, human activities must take on God's destiny for that city. This comes through the spreading of the gospel, the transformation of the minds of men. Deliverance ministries focus on inner healing and casting out demons, but they don't take part in direct combat. To free a city mankind must pass laws in accordance with scripture. Mankind becomes saved, born again, and transformed in such a way, that the laws in which govern the natural, mirror the laws that govern God's Kingdom. This is the beginning of heaven on earth!

Have you ever read or heard things like, as people function in signs, wonders, healings, and miracles, not deliverance, a breaking of the wickedness in the spirit realms happens. No, this is not true. What takes place? A person becomes healed, but if there is not the spread of the gospel and sinful establishments removed, then the Church experiences change but not the heavens. With most healing ministries, I have to go behind them and cast out demonic spirits and free people from fallen angels.

Miracles don't change atmospheres over cities, they help people to believe the gospel, desire to conform to the gospel, and that is the beginning to atmospheric transformation. We see this in the gospels and the book of Acts. God's healing power is not what dismantles the second heaven fallen angels and demonic spirits in regions of the earth. God's healing power touches the body, brings hope and faith to the spirit of man, but in most cases, that person is suffering from demons. The reason we do not see more people healed is that of demonic legal rights, curses, and strongholds. What dismantles and dethrones evil spiritual powers? The deliverance and healing ministry. The preaching of the gospel, with healing and deliverance taking place.

When deliverance is taking place, the minds of mankind become challenged or examined, and all kinds of thoughts take place within the minds of individuals. I have seen this for over 20 years. Deliverance will bring lies, doctrinal issues, divisions, and many other situations and excuses up. Deliverance forces the mind to see a righteous and holy God who is bringing the kingdom of darkness out into the open, yet the fallen angels at the same time are warring in the unrenewed places of the mind, trying to blind so they can't see God's glory in deliverance. Fallen angels are trying to convince mankind that deliverance need not take place, all the way too, manifestations of evil are not scriptural. Within those boundaries is how a christian can have a demon or their mind subdued by a fallen angel.

Most power ministries gravitate to the healing ministry. Why? Because deliverance unfolds and opens the kingdom of darkness to mankind. It reveals the minds of mankind. It shows who is in control, God or the fallen angels. It also brings slanderous accusations against ministries. Who is slandering? The fallen angels through the minds of the people who are obeying those evil thoughts and thus speaking. Power healing ministries believe they are making a difference in the breaking through the spirit realm over cities. To a small degree they are, but only giving people hope and faith through the healing the natural body, not freedom of the fallen angels and demonic spirits. Freedom is in the realm of deliverance. Healing ministries deal with the body, deliverance ministries deal with the soul and the mindsets of mankind. Many come to Christ through healing ministries, but most people stay demon possessed. Again, I have gone in behind these healing ministries and had to cast demons out of most of the people who Jesus has healed. In most cases, this is how they stay healed. Most people love healing ministries, but do not see the need or care about the deliverance ministry in the same light. This too is the work of the fallen angels. Let us not forget the simplicity of the gospel, the spirit is born again, the mind must be freed from the fallen angels, and the body must be delivered from demonic spirits, sickness, and sin. One last thing about the healing anointing. It can activate gifts of the Holy Spirit such as words of knowledge, but only the deliverance anointing free's mankind.

Authority Dethrones Fallen Angels

Only authority brings down the kingdom of darkness! With authority comes power. The more authority one has, the more power one can exercise. Authority is more important than power. Mankind conquers with power, but rules with authority. We see this in the book of Jude, verse 6. Angels, both good and evil, rule in sphere's of authority. They have a ruling authority which gives them the right to exercise a controlling influence through power. We also see this in Luke 4:31-37:

> *And He came down to Capernaum, a city of Gali-*
> *lee, and He was teaching them on the Sabbath; and*
> *they were amazed at His teaching, for His message*

was with authority. In the synagogue there was a man possessed by the spirit of an unclean demon, and he cried out with a loud voice, "Let us alone! What business do we have with each other, Jesus of Nazareth? Have You come to destroy us? I know who You are—the Holy One of God!" But Jesus rebuked him, saying, "Be quiet and come out of him!" And when the demon had thrown him down in the midst of the people, he came out of him without doing him any harm. And amazement came upon them all, and they began talking with one another saying, "What is this message? For with authority and power He commands the unclean spirits and they come out." And the report about Him was spreading into every locality in the surrounding district.
Luke 4:31-37

This is a perfect example of authority being exercised, and the result was power. Notice verse 36, the distinction of authority and power. It was the authority that gave Jesus the right to speak, and it was the power that drove out the demons. When we look at the word "Exousia," it means the highest judicial control. This refers to promotions to higher levels of authority until we reach Jesus' level. That is God's goal for us. It is clearly a supernatural force. Authority is a rightful, unimpeded power to act and exercise control over a jurisdiction. But power means physical power. Exousia or authority is the lawful right to act. In our scripture above, we see it was the power that drove out the demons, but it was the authority that gave Jesus the lawful right to act. Dunamis, the word for power, is creative, supernatural, miraculous strength. It is the means of change or the miraculous strength that drove out the demons.

Authority caused the demons to speak to Jesus. Notice one demon speaking for a group. This is authority, it drives up the demons. It also causes people to think well or ill of you. What did the demon mean by saying, "what business do we have with each other, Jesus of Nazareth?" A business is a person's occupation, profession, or trade. It is an activity that someone engages in. It is the work that one must accomplish or matters that have to be attend too. So business is the practice of making a living by earning a wage. This is key in the spirit realm. Demons earn spiritual wages to move up the demonic corporate ladder within their created status or level, to earn more spiritual power from the fallen angels who assign these tasks.

The demon speaking for all of them said, "I know who You are, the Holy One of God!" Demons know if you have authority or power, or if you have both. These demons knew Jesus was ruling with power. Ruling is the authority of the Kingdom of God. One must educate himself to rule before the lawful actions of power can be deployed. Deployment in the spirit realm is the movement of force or power so it establishes the kingdom of God. What did Jesus rebuke the demons for, their business? What does that mean in the celestial and terrestrial realms? Whatever wages these evil fallen angels and demons have earned must be transferred back to individuals, families, institutions, churches, cities, and regions!

In Acts 14:1-7 we see the miraculous power of God working and people came to the Lord:

> *And it came about that in Iconium they entered the synagogue of the Jews together, and spoke in such a manner that a great multitude believed, both of Jews and of Greeks. But the Jews who disbelieved stirred up the minds of the Gentiles, and embittered them against the brethren. Therefore they spent a long time there speaking boldly with reliance upon the Lord, who was bearing witness to the word of His grace, granting that signs and wonders be done by their hands. But the multitude of the city was divided; and some sided with the Jews, and some with the apostles. And when an attempt was made by both the Gentiles and the Jews with their rulers, to mistreat and to stone them, they became aware of it and fled to the cities of Lycaonia, Lystra and Derbe, and the surrounding region; and there they continued to preach the gospel. The Lockman Foundation. New American Standard Bible - NASB 1977 Modernized*

There was no unseating or dethroning fallen angels in Iconium. People were being saved, in fact a great number of Jews and Gentiles believed in Christ as the preaching of the gospel went forth. Take note, but the Jews who refused to believe stirred up the Gentiles and poisoned their minds. This is the work of the second heaven. Territorial fallen angels moved on the minds of the Iconium's, both Jew and Greek, and provoke them into anger. They stirred up thoughts of persecution in their minds, which led to desire. When we are doing the work of the Kingdom, and the minds of people in regions speak or treat you with hostility or ill-treatment, they are under the control and influence of the fallen angels of that region. This was the case in our scripture.

We recognize that God was saving souls through Paul and Barnabas. Paul and Barnabas spent a considerable amount of time in that region. This is stating that God only allowed the fallen angels limited access because the harvest was going on. God confirmed the message of the gospel with miraculous signs and wonders. As long as people continued to believe and minds changed, there will be a window in the heavenly realms for the harvest. When that window of time ran out through human choice, they conceived a plot to mistreat the apostles and stone them. The apostles realized it and fled to the cities of Lycaonia, Lystra and Derbe, and the surrounding region. They had to leave that territorial fallen angels jurisdiction. I know some of this may be new or hard to believe, but since 2007 I've been dealing with fallen angels and the minds of man.

The bible shows us that when we preach the gospel and God's grace is there for salvation and miracles, the devil and the fallen angels being the gods of this age, can blind the minds of humanity. The function of the fallen angels is to come down and defend their territory. It is the Churches job through prayer and fasting, worship and praise, holiness, evangelizing, and doing power ministry, to keep the window of God's grace open. If we train the leadership of the Church, this is when we can ask God for judgment of the territorial fallen angels. To have God judge them when they come into the earth or man's jurisdiction of authority. If we can recognize them when they come down, then God will move on the Churches behalf. This has happened so many times.

In Genesis 1:28 we see a powerful command to subdue the earth. What needed subduing? The fallen angels who fell before the creation of humanity. It was Satan, and the fallen angels who enticed Adam and Eve in the mind to transgress. It was a willful choice. With that decision came the surrender of the human mind. Without the surgical extraction of the fallen, this Evil Age, the fallen remain in the individual believers' minds. I don't like it, but those are the rules. The definition of subdue is to make subordinate. It means to conquer and control an environment. The Church has not learned to overcome and control, using Christ Jesus' authority and power to influence and direct the earth in which we live in. The Church has failed to subdue the fallen angels.

THE HEAVENS

When we speak of heaven, there is the single noun, heaven, which stress and highlights its overall unity and embodiment. There are other expressions that speak to its different features and or its levels. Words in the Bible like heavenlies or heavenly places suggest several places, levels, features, and realms of authority all under one heaven or one ruler, God the Father. Even the kingdom of darkness operates according to the laws established by God in the mid-heaven. For example, when there is righteousness in mankind, it binds evil's work. When there is sin, evil is free to express itself and to do its work according to the sins committed. In 2 Corinthians 12:2-4 Paul writes:

> *I know a man in Christ who fourteen years ago-whether in the body I do not know, or whether out of the body I do know, God knows-such a one was caught up to the third heaven. And I know such a man-whether in the body or out of the body I do not know, God knows-how he was caught up into Paradise and heard inexpressible words, which it is not lawful [or not possible] for a man to utter. 2 Corinthians 12:2-4*

The third heaven means the third in a series involving either time, space, or set of heavens. There are three heavens, and the definition says they are one above the other. Paul says God's dwelling place is in the third heaven and it is Paradise. On the cross, Jesus said to the repentant thief who asked Jesus to remember him, "Truly I say to you, today you shall be with Me in Paradise" (Luke 23:43 NASB). Paradise is God's dwelling and the most sacred place in the creation or universe.

There are heavenly places in the second heaven, four different levels of authority, with at least nine sub-levels or classes within each primary level. This is where the angels, both good and bad, fight for the right to control the lower dimensions. In the next chapter we will look more closely at those dimensions. With Jesus and Paul's accounts, what we do in the earth affects the heavenly realms. God designed heaven and earth to work together in unity. Therefore, God uses the miraculous! God's intentions are for the Church to operate in deliverance and healing. When miracles, deliverance, and healing are in operation, it changes the earthly or terrestrial moral order. When deliverance is effectively in operation, it changes the terrestrial and celestial or we could say; it changes all levels of the spirit realm. We must defeat the army of darkness, this is deliverance. Exposing the enemy to defeat them through spiritual warfare strategies that bring the collapse of fallen angels over cities.

The belief that the breaker anointing comes through healing, the prophetic, or any other anointing but deliverance, is revealing someone's lack of spiritual warfare. What moves and sets up the ability to break open the heavens is prayer? But prayer in its self does not break open the heavens. I know this statement could rub a lot of personal beliefs, but it is true. Let me explain! I was sent to a city in the heart of Texas. This city had a powerful healing ministry there for years, even before that, a prophetic and intercessory ministry. Before I could even hold my first service in that city, the second heaven showed up. These celestial fallen angels knew they had to stop my ministry. Why? Because the Holy Spirit does incredible deliverances through my ministry. This is the breaker anointing. I was to cast demons out of every person who had attended these healing and prophetic ministries. These people had attend these healing and prophetic ministries for years, yet when they came for deliverance night, I expelled demons, and fallen angels had to let them go. Here is a revelation that the body of Christ needs, just because you are saved, in this age you are still owned by the fallen angels through sin. Ouch! Again, if someone can't accept what I said, that in its self reveals the fallen angels over your family line and territory, who has blinded your eyes of understanding. Again, I don't like it, but since 2007 I've been in direct combat encounters that have proven this to be true. The sinful nature is that vehicle the fallen exploit. With my first encounter with Satan himself in spiritual warfare, it forced me to look deeper into the salvation and sanctification process. What I found was my spirit was borne again. My mind needed freedom from the fallen angels, the course of this age, and my body and emotions needed deliverance from demons because of sin. There is a deeper understanding to these truths I listed.

I have not run across one person who does not need deliverance. The reason for this conclusion is we don't understand the two unnamed characters in the New Testament called the old self and the new self. Therefore, I've placed these chapters in the middle of this book. We will never have a good balance and understanding of the New Testament if we don't theologically, personally, and supernaturally come to the deep truth's of these natures. Physically, I belong to this evil fallen age. Therefore, my body will die because of sin. Therefore, in this age of sin, the fallen have access to every human being through sin. I don't like it, but correct theology and encounter say it is so! Here is the good news, I can renew my mind and not allow the fallen angels access anymore. What I mean by access is the entrance into the mind of mankind. Peter was at one moment confessing revelation from God, then the fallen came down and Jesus had to rebuke Peter. This renewing is in accordance to the full mindset of Christ Jesus. Even with being caught up to the third heaven, Paul says he has not attained, but presses toward the goal of complete freedom in the mind and body from the fallen angels, demonization, and this evil Age.

Sin is the doorway that brought down Adam and Eve. Though Adam and Eve did not die immediately, sin brought a sentence of death, and worked in their lives as a curse. Like Adam, all of us who are descendants, do not die immediately upon sinning. We continue to live, enjoy countless blessing, but the evil fallen age is at work within, bring forth physical death. When the fallen angels sinned, they violated not only God's law and boundaries, but sinned against God. When the fallen caused Adam to sin, they came against God's image and likeness in humanity. This caused God to restrain the fallen angels to realms (pits) of darkness. The definition for hell here is to punish a sinner by sending him to a supernatural realm known for its darkness and bottomlessness or emptiness with torment. The fallen angels are still at work, unredeemable, waiting for the end of the millennium when their full judgment comes upon their heads. How do I know this, definition hints at it, but spiritual warfare confirms it? This revelation and the activity of high level fallen angels started to take place when I encountered the 24th created fallen angel from Satan. Same class, archangel, but his created order made him a little lower than Satan. He is a global player who carries falsely one name of Jesus. As I understand it today, I was free from his influence and his participation in directing the course of this evil age, but he still has legal rights in the earth according to mankind's breaking of God's laws. Let me say it this way, the one seeking freedom receives but all others remain captive. You may say, how is that possible? Or leaders have taught me that some evil angels are in a prison waiting judgment? In the book of Revelation 20:2, Satan, which is a person and a metaphor for the fallen angels, will be bound for a thousand years and then released for a short time. This is in line with Jude 6 which states that angels (which Satan is) who did not keep their own domain, but abandoned their proper abode, God has kept in eternal bonds under darkness. The fallen are bound to pits or realms of darkness, chained to a coming judgment. Let's look further, Revelation 20:2-3 states that Satan and his fallen angels will be bound. The definition is to tie objects together or tie these into bundles. Here is another clue to the rank and structure of the second heaven. These different classes of angels who operate accord to their created number, class, and realm, will be tied together as groups. More about numbers and ranks in the next chapter.

I have found that in most deliverance of the second heaven; it is the dismantling of the group. Working through the order seems to be the most effective. Though in the lower heaven of the second heaven, being able to get the one in charge to speak for his clan, and his subordinates going with him, works often as God's court determines, and even expelling all their demons who work for them. One thing I need to say here, Michael and his angels in Revelation 12 went into combat against Satan and his angels, they were not strong enough to stay in the heavenly realms; Michael defeated them, and cast them to the earth. Then the Church will engage in direct combat since the fallen angels have come down to man's realm of authority, defeat the fallen angels in such a way that causes the harvest and the return of Christ Jesus.

After over 10 years of combat with fallen angels, I firmly believe the power of the Holy Spirit will be so intense, the spiritual freedom that will come during the harvest of the last days will force a war in heaven and then on the earth. Will the Church undergo persecution, yes, will it be holy and full of glory, yes! With all these personal encounters, I believe they are only birth pains to the war coming for the souls of man!

Chapter Two

War In Heaven

A s we look at how the structure of the second heaven, I want to say, I don't have all the answers, but I can shed some tremendous light into this invisible structure which seems incredibly complex. We must always remember that evil is not something, but someone! Fallen angels are persons, we can say they are individual beings. They are created beings with angelic bodies they kept when they fell. Fallen angels on different levels have a wide range of intelligence and power, according to the dimension and the number of that dimension they were created for. Demons on the other hand are spirits without bodies. The Bible calls demons the nephilim or half breeds, the offspring of the fallen angels. This determines their wickedness and their intelligence. According to which fallen angel sired the demon, also determines their power. These series of books are not for the faint of heart, they are revelations of scripture slugged out in direct encounters that came through exorcisms.

The inscription Satan means "the one who resists or opposes." We know he is not just a person, but also a metaphor. So we can conclude, that it is the fallen angels who resists and opposes God, His purposes and God's people. We also know fallen angels slanderer and accuse. This happens in ministry sessions, they accuse the person and mankind for sin. They will reveal it to those who enter these power encounters they hate mankind. It is in these encounters that the minister must operate out of the fruit of the Holy Spirit.

Lucifer, now Satan, is one of the chief archangels and to my understanding, was in charge of one third the created angels. Therefore, God the Father will have them say things like, "I'm the 50th from Satan." Over time, God's promise to reveal the kingdom of darkness has come with these hints of bragging and pride. Through these many helpful hints and power encounters, Satan led his subordinates in pride and rebellion resulting in an insurrection. We see the mutiny in our sinful behavior, the desire to do it our way. It shows independence from God directly results from pride in some form of rebellion in mankind!

Following the forced ejection of one third of the angels, Satan and his fallen angels set up their own kingdom, so they may rule as they want too. This rebellious kingdom is in the mid-heaven or the second heaven. We learn from

Paul that this second heaven has four levels, thrones, then dominions, then principalities, and last or lowest, powers.

A throne is a seat, it is an actual chair of the state or a set of royalty, having a footstool or a world, continent, country, state, territory (multi-state), counties, cities, organizations, churches, individuals or rule. Notice that Paul says they are thrones, plural. What I know today, archangels depending on the order of their creation (the number system) and purpose for their creation (authority/power), sit over the Age/world (like Satan). In these descending orders of fallen archangels, they have authority over parts of this Age, over continents, countries, multi states, states, counties, cities, organizations, churches, families, and individuals. Each one of these stations or establishments have a tribunal or bench if you will; we could say elders. My findings in these tribunals is two-fold. One, God is the only One who is all knowing, so the fallen combine their intelligence. Two, they combine their efforts to draw power from the sins committed in the earth. Scripture talks about power in unity! The sins committed on the earth goes into the earth, and the fallen establish their rule.

> *"The earth is also defiled under its inhabitants, because they have transgressed the laws, changed the ordinance, broken the everlasting covenant." Isaiah 24:5 (NKJV)*

These high level fallen archangels like Satan, down through the descending orders, are influencing the minds of mankind to defile the earth by transgressing God's laws

(His Word), to break the ordinances of God, the way God designed man to live, and have broken the everlasting covenant or fellowship with God as Creator! So Isaiah 24:6 says,

> *"Therefore the curse has devoured the earth,*
> *And those who dwell in it are desolate.*
> *Therefore the inhabitants of the earth are burned,*
> *And few men are left."*

These evil archangel thrones draw power from sin, curses, and iniquities. Proverbs 29:2 states,

> *"When justice rules a nation, everyone is glad;*
> *when injustice rules, everyone groans." (CEV)*

My expanded version of Ephesians 6:12 says this: For our wrestling match is not against flesh and blood [contending only with physical opponents], not against persons with bodies, but against cosmic powers or fallen angels within four levels of the celestial realm who rule in various areas and descending orders of authority. Against world dominators of this present evil age, and against spiritual forces of wickedness in the heavenlies who are orderly tiered. Here is my explanation of my expanded version of the cosmic hierarchy:

This pictures a very highly structured organization of levels and grades according to numbers within a hierarchy who are well organized as a kingdom of four different dimensions in the second heaven. These different kinds of fallen angels within each of the four dimension have descending orders of authorities and different rulers and sub rulers according to grade and number responsible for different areas of authority in the second heaven which rule over the earth through the minds of mankind. For example the Bible lists, "great prince" Dan.12:1; "chief princes and princes" Dan 10:13. Daniel 10:13 is a very illuminating verse:

> *But the prince of the kingdom of*
> *Persia was withstanding me*
> *For twenty-one days; then behold, Michael,*
> *one of the chief princes, came to*
> *help me for I had been left there*
> *with the kings of Persia.*

I have underlined some keywords to the second heaven hierarchy. In medieval Latin from Greek, "hierarchy" was a system of ordered angels and or heavenly beings. We are talking about a system and organization in which angels are grouped and are ranked within their group according to their descending order. They are angels that have status, with authority and power to rule. Let me say it this way, they are arranged within a number system of classification according to importance. Michael a chief, but only one of the chief princes, came to give help, and assist in breaking the restraint or the legal rights to resist, that the prince of Persia owned. In power encounter ministry, after 10 years of operating in second heaven deliverance, angels that work for Michael or other Godly angels would say, I'm 12th in rank from Michael. As God brought down the fallen angels, only my background in exorcism gave me the ability to entertain through scripture this higher level of deliverance. Working with God's angels on such high levels and God's presence on those levels has helped me to understand this cosmic hierarchy.

Just the other day, I faced a fallen angel who was enthroned (throne/highest in the second heaven). His name was the "light bearer," and his main function was to twist the light of God as it shined through his (fallen angel) body. He had the right to stand in front of revelation truth and twist it because of unbelief. This high level archangel throne could blind the minds of men through choices. The "light bearer" seem to be able to deceive because the Church has not operated in the fruits of the Holy Spirit listed in Galatians 5:22-24 (NASB). Let us look at the scripture:

> But the fruit of the Spirit is love, joy, peace, patience, kindness, goodness, faithfulness, gentleness, self-control; against such things there is no law. Now those who belong to Christ Jesus have crucified the flesh with its passions and desires.

The battle was over the crucifixion of the sinful nature. He was one of the thrones over America. The "light bearer" claimed America wanted him, for the carnality of America calls out to him. The "light bearer" said he had legal rights because the Church was carnal and had not developed the fruits of the Holy Spirit which brings God's unrestrained power. He claimed the Church preaches a self based gospel. Instead of having the desire to see the fulfillment of the gospel within and throughout mankind, the Church preached a self satisfying gospel. This is just a very condensed version of what happened, but a glimpse into the way the fallen angels operate.

In dealing with individuals of the occult, they actually call Satan a prince, not a king. Kings are lower in rank in the second heaven. Now notice this closely, a fallen archangel who rules over Persia because of sin, was able to restrain, probably Gabriel an archangel until God sends Michael. Check this out! The fallen prince archangel over Persia called on his kings, his dominions if you will, and the equal of the lower rank matched the equal of the greater, so Gabriel was held up. Gabriel was left alone there with the kings of Persia. Let me give you an example, if you had a nickel, it would equal five pennies. In spiritual warfare in the heavenly realms, this happens all the time. These dominions equaled the geographical territory that the prince of Persia owned, and so Gabriel was left for twenty-one days, subdued until Michael a chief prince came. Why did Michael come, Daniel's prayers. I will talk about this more later in this chapter!

In scripture, the (NASB) Proverbs 15:22 says, "Without consultation, plans are frustrated, But with many counselors they succeed." Proverbs 24:6 says, "For by wise counsel you will wage your own war and in a multitude of counselors there is safety" (NKJV). Ecclesiastes 4:9, "Two are better than one because they have a more satisfying return for their labor." We can see there is power in unity, "one can chase a thousand and two ten thousand" (Deuteronomy 32:30). These are scriptural and supernatural principals. The higher the second heaven deliverance, the more the Church must come together in unity and prayer. Developing the fruit of the Spirit and preaching the gospel in a way that brings power.

As I understand it today, the different angels, good or bad, like the living creatures, seraphim, anointed cherub, cherubim, watchers, and all others who come under the hosts of heaven (all angels), all operate in the four levels of the second heaven. It is their status, number in rank, system and organization within each level. We could have a cherub of higher rank that is a throne or a cherub of lower rank called a dominion or they could be sub-rulers within those dimensions of thrones or dominions. Likewise, with principality and power. Their creation order by God determines their level, authority and power. Not all military Generals do the same things or command the same bases. What sets a four-star general apart from others, promotion date? This determines who is the senior in the room. My findings with Biblical scripture like sons of the Most High, the Bible calls them gods, but their job classification and rank are different. Fallen angels don't all act the same. Lower level powers, seem to toy or play with the minister to frustrate, as they did me the first time I encountered the fallen unknowingly. The lower level fallen can even appear as a demon to the untrained deliverance minister. Some higher ranking fallen angels look for the minister to come out of the posture of humility and scriptural court so they can strike with some legal judgment. We have been looking at Daniel 10, terror or a powerful presence of evil could appear when the fallen come down. Daniel remained humble and his focus was on the Lord and the glory touched Daniel.

We have talked about thrones! Next in the line of succession we have dominions! Dominions are lordships. In England, lords are a way of expression for prince or sovereign. In the United Kingdom the title today denotes a peer of the realm. From the different classes or created angels, dominions work for those who sit on thrones. Dominions also have sub-levels. They are more governmental over the jurisdiction of the thrones, much like lords who set in parliament over the realm of a king or queen. It is a title of honor expressive of respect. The Bible calls these realms, angelic majesties. Second Peter 2:11 says that God's angels don't speak evil of, they don't slander or accuse that brings reproach. Yet we hear Christian's address these fallen angelic majesties in such a way as to express rebuke. It is in a way of accusing them for their wrong, not realizing, that the sinful flesh of humanity is really the fallen angels nature in humanity and their legal right. Much like the United States has a President, Senate, and Congress, so like the dominions who govern for a throne. Again, each according to their creation number and status.

Principalities are much like governors. It really took over five years of investigation and combat to consider the definition and how this works. The Bible calls principalities the beginning or origin, the first one's, or first in a series. But principality can be used generically for any small monarchy, especially for a small sovereign state ruled by a monarch of a lesser rank than a king. Principalities seem to have a lot of control over regions. It seems they govern more over counties or we could say, multiple counties. They often have mountain ranges, rivers, etc... geographical markers as boundaries. Evil fallen principalities exercise first place in their rule of jurisdiction. Meaning they have liberty to establish their own evil government within that county, as long as it agrees with the thrones and dominions. In other words, they are to fulfill their assignment, but have liberty to exercise their own agenda. This is seen in the picture of America, and the picture of different cities, small or large; we could say, different make up or characteristics of different cities. Evil principalities can call on neighboring principalities or ask for a fallen angel above their rank for help if the Churches within that area starts to follow the early Churches pattern. Principalities, these are the first ones the Church must deal with. The principalities over cities and the fallen angel powers within the city. The goal of the Church is to establish righteousness which weakens the governing principalities or the group ruling over that city. Transformation of the way mankind lives and the laws established threaten the expulsion of those ruling evil fallen angels. Look again at Isaiah 24:5-6.

In the lower second heaven, fallen angels who are powers, really seem to effect the mental power of the human mind. They are very active in stirring up the minds of mankind, bringing the human mind under their control whose will and commands must be submitted to and obeyed. They are the doctrinal divisions, the abortion clinics and so on, through the minds a man. They are the fallen angels the occult people first seek out for power. These are your tarot card readers, psychic's, those who practice divination. They are also the cause of physical sickness that cannot be healed.

This happened in 2013, God spoke to me when I was shaving and said, "This Saturday (in four days), I want you to call this lady forward and ask Me to send down the fallen angel who owns the disease." This lady had Hypercoagulability or thick blood. Her sickness was progressively getting worse. When there is an imbalance in the proteins and cells responsible for blood and blood clotting develops, your blood can become too thick. After the message, I called her down and asked God to send down the fallen angel who owns the rights in the second heaven to her sickness. Immediately, God sent down the fallen angel and through direct combat of prayer (not confrontational deliverance), confrontational prayer, this evil fallen angel handed over the rights to the sickness. He was judged through confrontational prayer, and sent to tartaros. Once the judgment came, the lady was instantly healed. She was not able to get healed through any power healing ministries. There was a fallen angel out of mankind's dominion, the earth, in the second heaven, that we the Church needed to ask God to send him down for judgment so this believer could be healed. These powers, fallen angels, are the ones that keep most Christian's in deliverance ministry sessions for years. The believer just seems to never be free. It is a fallen angelic power, and it must be dealt with scripturally.

The Church must conclude that our battle is with fallen angels in the celestial realms and demonic spirits in the terrestrial realms. It involves the whole universe. Most believers are unaware who they are up against. Most believers don't have the experience to cast out high level demonic spirits, much less deal with the fallen angels. The Church focus' too much on the human sense realm, not the unseen realm. This is what the "light bearers" legal rights were. The outcome of the believer's focus for spiritual understanding will determine the results in every area of our lives and cities.

UNDERSTANDING THE REALM

In Mark 9:29, most believers don't have a clue what this single scripture really means. Think on this! If Jesus has given us authority in the earth to cast out demons so why should I pray and fast? I know from years of ministry, if I can't get the demon out, they have not met some condition, either on my part or the person's part who is getting ministry. I have authority on earth as long as I know what I'm up against. I must understand the realm I'm desiring to operate in. Authority is the right to act. Power is the strength to subdue. So when I act in authority, power is there to enforce my rightful actions. The key word in Mark 9:29 is "kind." This kind, meaning a different kind of spirit. The definition has to do with a category or class, based upon an implied derivation and/or lineage. The lineage here is a paternal kin or a family member. It is a different race, stock, class or species! This kind means a category of beings distinguished by some common characteristic and qualities. What is the common characteristics and qualities of demons and fallen angels, evil! In Mark 9, just like the lady with thick blood, mentioned above, nothing was happening until Jesus dealt with the second heaven. Most believer's error in their thinking and preaching, saying the disciples did not have enough faith. Ask yourself this question, we're the disciple acting? Then what was wrong? They were clueless about this kind of evil spirit, the fallen. Until this power encounter, Jesus only introduced the disciples to demonic spirits, terrestrial warfare. Jesus tells them by His statement, "This kind come out only by prayer." In today's language, fallen angels are to be dealt with through power encounter prayer. The lack of breakthrough shows the lack of understanding, not unbelief.

I have experienced this very thing. Understanding causes us to act in authority, and that's seen through power! Jesus dealt with a fallen angel in the region, probably a fallen angelic power, showing how the soon to be Apostle's should go about establishing the Kingdom. When a believer is casting out evil spirits, and nothing really is happening, it probably is the lack of understanding or biblical conditions have not been met or there is a different level of warfare, and we must develop new tactics. In Matthew 17:20, little faith has to do with not enough faith. Until we are clued in to the realm we must operate in, faith will never be there. I can't have faith until I have the opportunity to understand truth! Faith comes by hearing the Word of God. The disciples needed to hear Jesus!

WAR WITH ANGELIC MAJESTIES

Those who are experiencing God judging fallen angels coming down from the celestial realm to the terrestrial realm, understand the vast, or multi-levels of the second heaven. These different levels have descending orders within each of them. As stated in my book series, the second heaven has four main levels, and within each level, there are nine sub-levels or class of fallen angels as I know it today. There are many different kinds and classes of fallen angels, who have many descending orders of authority is my point. The second heaven fallen angels rule in various areas, and these spiritual dignitaries rule through the minds, the sinful nature and acts of mankind. Paul states in Colossians 1:16 NASB 1977:

*"For by Him all things were created, both in the
heavens and on earth, visible and invisible,
whether thrones or dominions or rulers or
authorities, all things have been created by
Him and for Him."*

To effectively defeat these fallen angels, we must know who, where, what, and how. It's one thing to pray for individuals, because it is the sins and iniquities in the family line back to Adam that is warred over by the second heaven. But the war is also over the sins committed on the land. So over regions and family bloodlines, we must pray for God to move throughout our area, for the awakening to begin, and power evangelism to consume the Churches.

In Ephesians 2:2, Paul states that Satan is called the prince of the power of the air. Satan is the highest of the evil princes, but there are many princes of fallen angels enforcing Satan's rule. These high level princes are ordering first thrones, second dominions, third principalities, and fourth powers, to steer the course of this age. These fallen angels work in groups or clans in spiritual regions defined as "air." There are two Greek words for "air." The first word, "aither," denotes the higher elevated atmosphere and is never applied to the second air touching the earth's surface. My point here is that the fallen angels under Satan's rule, claim dominion over the entire surface of the earth, yet rule from the celestial realm.

When I take into account Daniel 10 and Colossians 1, I am given a glimpse of the multi-leveled or tiered structure and activity that goes on through spiritual warfare. Through scriptures like these, I have come to understand that there are many different levels (nine as of today) within the four dimensions of the second heaven. There are many classes of angels, both fallen and God's holy angels who are tiered within each dimension of the second heaven. I cannot repeat myself enough! Also, God's angels seem to operate in both the second heaven and in the third heaven. It is prayer that starts the conflict, like Daniel. Prayer for God's desired plan for mankind begins a generational war that is to be fought until the return of Christ. When prayer has taken root within a body of believers, then the wrestling match between the fallen angels and the Church starts for the souls of mankind. What I mean by taking root, the majority of that assembly begins to pray. Depending on how the Church operates together over regions, determines what class of warfare will take place. I have also found that prayer invokes combat in the second heaven between God's holy angels and the fallen angels. It is the failure of the Church to pray without ceasing that has kept the fallen angels enthroned. This is one of the greatest revelations that I have found in second heaven combat. The Churches job is to force these cosmic fallen angels to physically come down to defend their various levels and jurisdictions of rule in the earth. What causes the fallen to come down, the freeing of mankind through prayer, power evangelism, and deliverance. When people are getting saved, the Church must not bring them into the congregation until the saved have been water baptized, endued with the power of the Holy Spirit (speaking in tongues), and exorcised of demons and fallen angels. When the fallen come down and the peoples minds are set free, then they are ready to enter the congregation of the Lord.

Ephesians 6:12 – For our wrestling match is not against flesh and blood [contending only with physical opponents], not against persons with bodies, but against cosmic powers and or fallen angels who rule within various areas and descending orders of authority. Against world dominators of this present darkness, against spiritual forces of wickedness in the heavenlies.

This pictures a very highly structured and well organized kingdom with fallen angels in the second heaven and demonic spirits in the earth who have descending orders of authorities and different rulers and sub rulers responsible for different areas of authority in the second heaven and on earth.

Let us actually work through Paul's account of spiritual warfare. First is the word 'our'! This refers to something that will be done throughout this evil age. It will be the Churches and the Christian's struggle with the levels of the devil's kingdom. Wrestling is a contest between two in which each endeavors to throw the other, and which is decided when the victor is able to hold down his opponent with his hand upon his neck. In wrestling, the control of the neck and head is everything. This is why the person going through fallen angel deliverance feels their neck tighten up and their head or mind feel oppressed in different manners. This definition is a match or a contest in which individuals, teams, and people compete against each other. This is what Paul is wanting the Church to come to the knowledge of. This contest between the multi-facets of the kingdom of darkness and God's Church is a military campaign that will involve the act of engaging in close hand-to-hand combat as this evil age exists.

We do not wrestle against humanity, but with fallen angels who have cosmic power in the second heaven within various areas of the earth. Paul is speaking about humanity having mental struggles and emotions that can bring different levels of mental suffering. This mental suffering is from the fallen angels; those thoughts of continual or seasonal bombardments of the mind over destinies, callings, or gifting. The design is to twist the truth so that the one would believe the lie. The lies in the mind are arranged in such a way as to cause the person to give up and not pursue God's plan for their life. To twist is too distort so that the fallen angels can make a mockery of the individual or Church. These revelations are not only biblical definitions, but definitions explained through power encounters. Fallen angels desire to interlace or weave their thoughts into the minds of humanity in order to steer and control the movement and course of this evil age. So, we are not warring against persons with bodies, but against the mental mindsets of humanity that are controlled by fallen angels who have ordered the possession of humanity with demons. When the fallen angels order and send the demonic, they will protect the demonic. This has happened many times in demonic exorcism. Fallen angels are committed to certain demonic spirits remaining in the family bloodline for the control of generations to come, so they come down to block the deliverance. Remember, this is an army who is committed to removing God from His own creation.

What is the definition of a fallen angel? The fallen are defined as first ones, preeminent ones or leaders. They are chief or first in time, meaning the creation. The fallen are the beginning, meaning the ones who sinned first and began this fallen evil age. They call themselves "fallen" and the definition states that they are ancient ones, kings, captains, princes. The Bible says they are angelic majesties or celestial beings. They are dignitaries in exalted positions. The fallen consider themselves to be important because of their high rank and office in the original creation. In no way are they demons or demonic principalities. Demonic principalities are not scripturally defined and those that speak or write about that statement, speak and write out of presumption. The body of Christ has had enough idea's that one believes to be true, but is not. Let us not adopt a particular attitude or belief or statement, until we have had enough power encounters to rightfully divide the scriptures. I do understand what these writers are referring to, but within the statement demonic principalities, it could give some belief of false authority and power.

So the heavens and the earth were completed, and
all their hosts (inhabitants). Genesis 2:1 Amplified

The inhabitants the Bible is referencing are angelic armies. The definition calls them angelic troops according to their order and number. This multi-leveled army of warfare are very well organized and cover the whole creation within each of its dimensions. These angelic armies are both light and darkness. One fights on the command of God the Father, the other fights on the command of the ruling throne within that jurisdiction. These evil thrones, dominions, principalities, and powers are extremely dark and evil. They have incredible strength and power. Isaiah 40:26 says that God brings out their host or angel armies by number. Isaiah is referring to God's angel armies and notice they are numbered. Remember, Satan lead a rebellion and one third of the angels fell, describing this age. This numbering system that I have found seems to point to the number of soldiers the kingdom of darkness has summoned to stand against. In many power encounters, these evil fallen angels come forward for judgment, and announce their rank and position within the number system.

In Matthew 12:29 Jesus speaks of a strongman's house. This house is a dwelling that serves as his living quarters for one or more families. The strongman refers to the ruling fallen angel over his jurisdiction of authority. Jude 9 speaks of area's of authority. The families that the definition is talking about is the sub-rulers that help enforce his domination over the territory. Whether the strongman is a demon within the human body, or all the way to Satan as the god of this evil age, it is all about control for territorial right through righteousness or sin.

Bible commentator F.F. Bruce somewhere in his writings states that the Septuagint reading of Deuteronomy 32:8 is as followers:

> *When the Most High gave to the nations their inheritance, when He separated the children of men, He set the bounds of the peoples according to the number of the angels of God. Deuteronomy 32:8 (Septuagint)*

Again the word number comes forward. With more than one thousand power encounters with fallen angels, I have found that within each fallen rulers geographical territory, the fallen angels are numbered according to their rank of creation first, and according to their position of authority within that territory second. When we examine the Septuagint translation of Deuteronomy, we see a global reign first, a national reign second, and individual territories within each nation. This also I find true through power encounters with fallen angels. One of the definitions of hosts in Genesis 2:1 is, heavenly entourage. Like I have found in demonic deliverance, I also have found in fallen angel deliverance, they run in groups. The group, clan, or entourage of fallen angels seem to work together, pooling their intelligence and power. They seem to work as a counsel plotting how to fulfill their assignment given from those above them, and ordering those below them. The princes over nations seem to order the kings, and the kings over a smaller nation or states seem to order the captains over territorial land markers as rivers, mountain ranges down to state county lines. There are Chief Princes, Princes, Kings, and Captains in this order. But each chief prince has sub-ruling chief princes, and so on. This is why it took 10 years of unraveling, and I only feel that I've just scratched the surface. Some fallen angels are territorial, some are over institutions (Masonic Lodge) for example, some if allowed over Churches, and some over bloodlines and so on.

Remember before what I said, this pictures a very highly structured and well organized kingdom of fallen angels in the second heaven who have descending orders of authorities and different rulers and sub rulers responsible for different areas of authority in the second heaven and on earth.

The houses of Jerusalem and the houses of the kings of Judah will be defiled like this place, Topheth, all the houses on whose rooftops incense has been burned to all the host of heaven (sun, moon, stars), and where drink offerings have been poured out to other gods. Jeremiah 19:13 Amplified

Jeremiah is stating that the celestial bodies as heavenly host became the object of pagan worship. In the Old Testament, the heavenly bodies and the angel armies references seem to merge. The two meanings of the Hebrew phrase for "host of heaven" reflect an association between angels and stars and planets in Hebrew imagination and writing. If there is some association between angels and stars, and planets according to the Hebrew, notice very carefully Genesis 1:16,

> *God made the two great lights—the greater light (the sun) to rule the day, and the lesser light (the moon) to rule the night; He made the [galaxies of] stars also [that is, all the amazing wonders in the heavens]. Genesis 1:16 Amplified*

Notice they were created in groups and in orders according to the creation account! This to I find in power encounters. Remember Paul in Colossians 1:16, visible and invisible. God, in calling this hidden army "the stars," the Bible is calling upon ancient identifications of angelic armies.

> *Then Micaiah said, "Therefore hear the word of the Lord: I saw the Lord sitting on His throne, and all the host of heaven standing by, on His right hand and on His left. 1 Kings 22:19 NKJV*

In Psalm 82, these fallen angels are called "sons of God" or "sons of the Most High." Job 38:7 they are called "sons of God" or "morning stars." Each different in class, rank, creation, grouped but numbered. In 1 Kings 22:19-23, I point to the military strategy being discussed and a fallen angel coming forward to be a deceiving spirit in the mouths of all Ahab's prophets. This fallen angel had to be high enough in the structure to influence the nation.

I don't want anyone to miss what is happening here! When God foresaw the nations and predetermined their inheritance, He established angels over the creation and in descending orders. God assigned angelic armies over the creation, nations, states, counties, cities, institutions, and family bloodlines and or people groups. Jeremiah said the Hebrews knew of these gods or fallen angels and worshipped them. God placed angelic armies throughout the heavens and the earth. There is nothing created that God did not assign angels over. When one third sinned and fell, these fallen angels kept their positions of authority, like us, it was their nature that changed. Just let me add here, if you believe that fallen angels are high level demons, then I know you have never encounter them in spiritual warfare. The very minute someone talks to a fallen angel like a demon, is the minute their life is in jeopardy. Go and read my first book called, "Exploring Secrets of the Heavenly Realms/Mysteries of the Second Heaven Explained.

DANIEL'S PRAYER

As we look again at Daniel 10, we find Daniel in a state of mourning and fasting some 21 days. Remember what Jesus said, this kind only comes out by prayer and fasting. Comes out of what? The Mind! Daniel has been moved by

God in deep sorrow because of the desolation of the city of Jerusalem.

In those days I, Daniel, was mourning three full weeks. I ate no pleasant food, no meat or wine came into my mouth, nor did I anoint myself at all, till three whole weeks were fulfilled. Daniel 10:2-3

As Daniel pursued an answer from God, Gabriel an archangel who was lower in rank than Michael, was visited. Let us also remember before we get too far, that Daniel 10-12 are a single continuous revelation of events. What is in play here? The future of Israel. It was Daniel's desire to know what God was going to do with Israel. Israel had been departing Babylon, and Daniel's heart was heavy over the rebuilding programs of the temple and wall.

As Daniel sets himself in prayer, one righteous man, through prayer and fasting, unleashes a cosmic battle that involves Chief Princes, Princes, and Kings of the highest angelic order. This battle was not only over Israel's future, but for prophetic time itself. Even the duration of Persia was on the line. Daniel was given a revelation that concerned a great war! Daniel's prayer was heard the first day, but Gabriel had to pass through the second heaven. Gabriel was withstood or opposed by an evil archangel called the Prince of Persia, and was detained or held captive by an equal force, the kings (plural) of Persia. This is an archangel fight! Some of these archangels were of higher rank than the others. Some of these lower enthroned archangels were called kings. There seem to be enough kings there to equal the archangel Gabriel as I said before. This too I find in power encounters, and must ask God for higher ranking angels to bring breakthrough. These fallen evil enthroned archangels war against God's enthroned archangels, a cosmic battle of epic proportions. The Prince of Persia was to resist God's angels and to enforce his reign over the kingdom of Persia. Today is no different.

Remember, the definition for archangels is chief rulers or princes. I also commented a few pages ago that the princes over nations seem to order the kings, and the kings over a single nation seem to order the captains over territories. I also want to say, that there is one ruling archangel over a nation with many other sub-ruling archangels over that nation. This battle took place because one prophetic intercessor felt the heart of God and humble himself for God's will. Just think what the Church could do with a heart like Daniel.

Let us look at one more class of angelic majesty according to scripture, the rank of captain. In Joshua 5:14, the NKJV says, 'so He said, "No, but as Commander of the army of the Lord I have now come."' Yet the Amplified says, 'He said, "No; rather I have come now as captain of the army of the Lord."' Joshua's battle was for Jericho, a city within a territory. The King James uses the word 'captain' also. In the first few pages of this chapter I said, "this pictures a very highly structured organization of levels and grades according to numbers within a hierarchy." I also commented on Chief Princes, Princes, King's and Captains, this is just a small breakdown of the good and evil angelic structure.

Joshua's eyes are opened to an angel of God who has the rank of captain, and is in command of an angelic army. This captain has a message for Joshua. He instructs Joshua that Jericho will be delivered into Joshua's hands. He is to march around the city once with all the armed men, for six days. Joshua is to have seven priests carry trumpets and rams' horns in front of the ark. On the seventh day they are to walk around Jericho seven times with the priests blowing the trumpets and on the long blast of the trumpet, the army was to give a long loud shout so that the walls would collapse. We have the visible and the invisible here. The minute Joshua and Israel obeyed God, the invisible war of the angelic armies started. The war between the captain and his army verses the territorial fallen angel captain and his army within the geographical regions of Jericho. After the invisible army of darkness was defeated, God ordered the captain to have his army destroy the stronghold or knock down the wall. This is why prayer walking our cities is so important. Logging places of sin and praying for a move of God. Power evangelizing those areas that have been prayer walked. We must prayer walk and power evangelize until the breakthrough starts. Once the breakthrough comes, then we attack with the full force. We target Christian businesses to go and do power evangelism within the prayer walked boundary, and God answers with signs and wonders. -

Chapter Three

Spiritual Warfare

There is so much material out there stating we have been born into a war as Christians. This warfare is between the kingdom of darkness and the kingdom of light. Yet, there is very little material on the vast size and the enormous undertaking that faces the body of Christ. Some tell us through messages and or books, all kinds of beliefs and methods about spiritual warfare. For example, some say a demon cannot possess a christian. Others say the demons attach themselves to people. Even others say we are not to confront evil or that curses don't affect or influence Christians. There are many beliefs like this! I'm not sure how people come up with these theories, for it is plain in scripture we must deal with everything listed above. Christians do and most have demonic possession, curses, and legal rights through the flesh and their generations. There are two deliverance ministries that have world anointing's on them. One has gone to be with the Lord, Derek Prince. The second is Bob Larson. He is still casting out demons. Both are legitimate high level anointing's, but are completely different. As any student of the Bible should, I have taken both ministries and combined them into my ministry. By doing this, God has promoted me. What I took from their (Derek/Bob) generation, I have built upon, and now God has me dealing with second heaven fallen angels in which they do not. So, let us look at some scripture and find balance through truth!

In Luke 11:24-26, Jesus states when an unclean spirit goes out of a man! First, Jesus does not make a distinction between different kinds of men, saved or unsaved. Jesus simply says the evil spirit exits, or goes out of. The definition puts it many ways, like to go away from or to depart; even to be separated from. But I like J.P. Louw and E.A. Nida's definition. It means to move out of an enclosed or well defined two or three dimensional area, to leave from within. Even the biblical definer Strong's says the unclean or evil spirit departs out of a place or expelled or is cast out. William Mounce, in his dictionary of old and new testament words says, to cast out is to drive out, and it often indicates a violent expulsion. Does that sound like the evil spirit is attached or within? Does that sound like if we get close enough to Jesus, they will just leave? Does that sound like the truth of God's Word would just set us free without expulsion? Here's a fact, we know that demons don't enter unless there is a curse and or a legal right. We also know how to divide the Word of God correctly as in Ezekiel 18:1-2 talking about generational curses, and then shifting the conversation to each individual being responsible for decisions and actions from verse three onward. These are the simplicities of the Word of God.

If you and I can really wrap our mind around the New Testament, we quickly find out that our spirit man, if born again, belongs to the Age to Come. Jesus makes this point so clear, and without question in the gospel of John, chapter 3. We know from Romans 12 that our mind is being renewed or slowly renovated, restored so we can operate as believers in this evil age, out of the power of the age to come. The epistles tell us that our body is dead because of sin, or we could say it belongs to this evil age and the god of this age. Why do you think the devil was arguing with Michael over the body of Moses. Again, the simplicity of the gospel is always best. So our body belongs to this evil age because of sin and the curse, death! The simple truth is, our body, the flesh, responses to this evil age. The condition of the flesh, belongs to the fallen angels and Satan who are the gods of this evil present darkness.

The gospel tells us that when Jesus comes to establish the millennium, we who believe in Christ Jesus will receive perfected sinless bodies. At that time our bodies will respond to the age to come. We will talk more about the old self and the new self in a later chapter. But, if we don't understand our two self's, then we believe and make statements like a Christian cannot be demonized or demons are attached or believers can't be cursed or Christians are completely set free upon salvation. Thought processes like these fail to understand positional and conditional Christianity, and by way of personal belief, deny the message of the New Testament about the old self and new self.

What did Louw and Nida mean in their definition as to move out of an enclosed two or three dimensional area? First, demons and fallen angels affect the mind and the body. Two truths here, demons consider human bodies their home and desire to operate through the human will and emotions. Fallen angels consider the minds of men their possession and do not seek bodily possession as do demons to do their work. Fallen angels have bodies, where demons are disembodied spirits. For more on this subject, see my first book called, "Exploring Secrets of the Heavenly Realms."

So a two and or three dimensional area of demonization is tiered within a person and or within family members. The same demon in one family member could be in all family members, especially if it is a generational demon, this is dimensional. That same demon with his group who works for him, could also be tiered or have a series of levels, especially if it is generational in the person or family. This is what Louw & Nida is defining as two dimensional. But the third dimension adds a component or element of a larger picture. There are certain demons that come and go from people or family members. They too are usually tiered, but have the right to travel to other members of the family. Yet also have to right to possess all of the family at once.

When we are talking about dimension, examples are always helpful. Let me give you an example! As light passes through a prism, the light will break up into many component colors. Let me say it this way! Since we are talking about the third dimension, light passing through a triangular prism causes different wavelengths of light, to disperse, leaving the prism at different angles, creating a rainbow effect. Let us say the light of the sun enters a triangular prism, reflecting red, orange, yellow, green, blue, indigo, and violet, the colors of the rainbow. Just as you can only see a rainbow if the Sun is behind you and the rain is in front of you, unless this truth is understood, effective deliverance cannot take place. What truth? The truth that most demons are tiered and they are dimensional.

In that truth of the third dimension, the demon looks to set up many levels, much like the many colors of the rainbow. There is also one other element to these dimensions. Demons have the ability to fragment or to separate off, upon being cast out. This too I find in Biblical definition. Remember the definition, to be separated from. The demons being cast out are looking for something incomplete in the ministry session that they can break or fragment into. Evil spirits operate in dimensions that we don't, so the importance of learning and biblical understanding comes through power encounters. Simply put, a part of the whole demon is left or we could say, a piece of the whole is left and a doorway is created for re-entry. Evil spirits have to give over ground taken in the deliverance session, but if not all is covered, it is like owning one acre of land, and part of it not cleared for living purposes.

Why do demons fight like this and split off, hoping to come back through that door? Because upon expulsion they travel on a spiritual road which leads to hell, the pit. Their journey takes them through regions of hell, the different levels of hell or the pit, until they reach their assigned torment, for the evil they have done. The expelled demons go through dry places, down into Hades, to the underground prison of punishment. The expelled demons then say, the house or human body is empty, swept, and put in order, I will return. Through that doorway of not finishing different dimensions of deliverance or a return to sin, because the person has not pursued holiness and grew in the Word of God, and sought total freedom, those demons are allowed to come back and bring more wicked ones with them. The number seven is one of the most significant numbers of the Bible because it is the number of spiritual perfection. Seven is the number which is stamped on every work of God. So, the total amount of demons that come back are in accordance to how God worked or what He did for you, and the lack of spiritual pursuit on our part. This is no joke! Our lack of gratefulness, plus the amount of God's grace that brings freedom, equals the total amount of repossession. What causes this repossession? Sin or unwillingness to finish!After the expulsion, there is a period of rest, but most don't understand, the amount of sin in one's old life, plus the length of time in those sins, equals the amount of deliverances one needs. These are facts of time-tested ministry and my spiritual father's training I have received. After 20 years of ministry, this is the simplest and most truthful answer.

CHAPTER THREE

People going through deliverance must understand the battle or wrestling match within. The pursuit of freedom will get harder if one does not get ministry quickly when the inward battle begins again. The thoughts will come, the desires will also come. There seems to be an unwillingness for one to say, I need another ministry session during their walk to freedom. Why? The evil spirit convinces the individual that everything is now fine.

The one who continues in their freedom will go through an inward battle that becomes so intense, the shift or balance of the war inside the mind is turning for the person who is desiring to be free. The evil spirits inside are losing the war, losing ground, and the evil army is being dismantled. So there must be a full onslaught or counterattack. When this is the case, I recommend an intense, a 8 hour deliverance session. I call this all out war! I have even had 3 days of 8 hours with people. We go until the enemy is now on the retreat!

As we close Luke 11:24-26, notice in Jesus' teaching, He says the demon calls our body his house. Doesn't that sound like demonization? Strongs Dictionary says a house is an inhabited house or home. It is a dwelling place of the human body as where the abode of demons possess. The key words here in the definition is human body! Jesus says the last state of that man will be worse than the first. Jesus means in a temporal succession or that which remains after the rest have been conquered. After the demons return to their home and reclaim their territory, there seem to be a chronological order of events according to Jesus that causes in process a continuous giving away to another; that is the more wicked than himself. I find this definition also to be true in combat with evil spirits. The temporal is this evil age! The demons that we're cast out, come back and repossess the human body, and the more wicked come to create an order of events that cause deeper possession and a continuing takeover for new ground. This too I have seen so many times. People becoming worse off because of falling back into the same sin, and even more or deeper sin!

WRESTLING WITH EVIL PROPERLY

Let's look in the last Chapter at Ephesians 6:12 in both the NASB and my expanded version:

> *For our struggle is not against flesh and blood, but against the rulers, against the powers, against the world forces of this darkness, against the spiritual forces of wickedness in the heavenly places. (NASB 1977)*

My Expanded Version: For our wrestling match is not against flesh and blood [contending only with physical opponents], not against persons with bodies, but against cosmic powers or fallen angels within four levels of the celestial realm who rule in various areas and descending orders of authority. Against world dominators of this present evil age, and against spiritual forces of wickedness in the heavenlies who are orderly tiered. Here is my explanation of my expanded version of the cosmic hierarchy: This pictures a very highly structured organization of levels and grades according to numbers within a hierarchy who are well organized as a kingdom of four different dimensions in the second heaven. These different kinds of fallen angels within each of the four dimension have descending orders of authorities and different rulers and sub rulers according to grade and number responsible for different areas of authority in the second heaven which rule over the earth through the minds of mankind.

I want us to start by focusing on the word struggle or wrestle as the NKJV translates it. This word wrestle, shows us just how intense spiritual warfare must end up. It is nice to go through repentance, renouncing legal rights, curse breaking, and non-confrontational deliverance, but eventually, there must be a showdown.

The word wrestle is from the old Greek "pale," meaning a struggling, wrestling, or hand-to-hand combat. We also know from the Greek, "pale" is where the Greeks derived the word "Palaestra." Palaestra was a huge palace of combat sports located in the center of the city. What does this reveal to us in the invisible realm? We see many different kinds of sports or different kinds of spiritual warfare. This shows the believer that there will be many Christian struggles with the different kinds of evil, and the multi-layered powers of evil. One of the definitions from the Lemma is a school of wrestling and exercise. The Christian soldier must understand that on the outside, the "Palaestra" looked like a palace, but on the inside it was a school of war. This is a picture of how most believers look. On the outside, they look like their Christian life is all together, but on the inside, they are at war! Most don't know where these intense mental and emotional struggles come from.

The majority of believers choose to deny that evil resides within them. They choose not to believe that dwelling within their mental and emotional state, evil spirits occupy and possess parts of them. These evil spirits can be so engrafted within the persons personality, that they actually believe this is who they are. Yes, most believers engage in some form of intense struggles through vices, and these vices should make known to them that evil forces are warring within their members, the palace. The stronger the opposition in the will of man, or the realm of temptation, the greater the evil spirit. It is the saints responsibility to mature and understand that what is unseen, is seen in emotions and behavior, righteousness or sin. Whether we war inside through our mind, will, emotions, or we are at war outside through persecution, unbelief, or oppressive behaviors of others, Paul says it is not against flesh and blood, persons without bodies.

In Roman times, these dedicated athletes, cultivated their skills, morning, afternoon, and night. They were very committed, determined, and brave athletes of their time. This dedication of working out and training was to be respect by all that watched. Because of what these athletes do, they were housed in a palace. Can you picture the invisible realm and what Paul is referring too. Paul is saying that fallen angels and demons are dedicated, work continually, and are ready to defend their palace, the human body and places in the parts of the unrenewed mind.

CHAPTER THREE

There were three primary or kinds of athletes, boxers, wrestlers, and those of combat sport. This shows those who do deliverance that there are different kinds of demons and fallen angels. Boxers in the first century, they were not like boxers today. They were the most feared, because it was extremely violent. Boxing of that time involved such physical damage, that they were made to wear protective helmets. Very few boxers ever lived long enough to retire, most died in the ring. These first century boxers wore gloves with steel blades and nailed spikes sticking out, in order to make deep gashes in the opponents skin. Most of the ancient Greek boxers faces, ears, and noses were deformed. Boxers of that time had no rules, it was hand-to-hand combat, no rounds to stop and rest. It went on until one of the two surrendered or died in the ring.

Wrestling of the first century was a contest between two in which each endeavored to throw the other, and able to hold his opponent down with hands upon his neck to be declared the victor. It was extremely physical and exhausting.

The Greek word for the third sport is "pankratos." In this sport, anything goes, no part of the human body was off limits. They could kick, gouge, punch, bite, break bones, and other horrible things to win.

We as Christians cannot deny what the Apostle Paul was alluding too, a picture of a very highly structured organization of levels and grades according to numbers within a hierarchy who are well organized and trained, ready to defend their palace. This picture is of a war that would be a spiritual fight, to face the enemy in confrontational deliverance and defeat them. To some evil spirits, the fight is their ownership of parts of the human body and mind to defend. To others, it is this evil age. To all evil in-between, they are only defeated by those believers who are trained better than they. Jesus and Paul's instructions were to attack these palaces or strongholds, and to pull them down through skillful understanding and power encounters. Notice what Paul says in Second Timothy 2:24-26 (NASB):

The Lord's bond-servant must not be quarrelsome, but be kind to all, able to teach, patient when wronged, 25 with gentleness correcting those who are in opposition, if perhaps God may grant them repentance leading to the knowledge of the truth, 26 and they may come to their senses and escape from the snare of the devil, having been held captive by him to do his will.

Paul instructs us to present the truth with godly Christian character and in a way that some may change their mind. No one can do this for them. In spiritual warfare, the person must come to their senses. They must have the revelation that parts of them that sin have been trapped. They have been caught like a bird entangled in a net. What is that net? Whatever sin and vice that is bringing peril, loss, sickness, and destruction. The snare is seen through allurements and seductions of sin. These allurements or seductions, once acted upon, the fallen angels and demons have legal rights to hold that person captive. Like a mouse trap baited with cheese. The mouse is lured through the senses, tempted to take what appears to be good, but the trap is set and designed to bring forth death.

To be held captive Paul says, is someone who has been taken alive and made a prisoner of war. The definition is to catch and capture alive. Like that mouse who's head is held down by that trap, captured, is now undergoing the death process. This is the design of demon possession and fallen angel activity, to bring forth death.

In the Roman world, war and slavery went hand in hand. It was slavery being the inevitable outcome of defeat in a combat encounter. The person giving in to sin. One soldier was overcome by the other, and made a prisoner of war, spoils Jesus says! Captivity is designed to bring forth death. But make no mistake about it, the prisoner and their generations are to be held captive in the mind and body until the age to come. Every generation is held in this manner until one generation breaks free and fights not only for themselves, but for future generations.

Romans made their prisoners march under an arch made of three spears fastened together. This was a symbol of their defeat and was known as "passing under the yoke." Many times, I have people says they feel like their neck and shoulders hurt or feel tense in deliverance. They have passed under the ache, the ache fallen angel and his demons that have brought imprisonment. This was a Roman metaphor for harnessing the beasts. What Paul is telling Timothy, those who oppose have been taken alive as captive by the devil, fallen angels, and demonic spirits to do their bidding.

Through the sinful nature, we are born into the kingdom of darkness service. We serve their pleasure, sin. Once becoming born again, our spirit starts to respond to God, coming to the realization that our minds must be renewed and set free. There is a difference of the mind set free, verses renewed. The human mind must be set free from the fallen angels, where the mind renewed must take on the mind or thinking patterns of Christ Jesus. Most believers do not understand the difference. Again, see my first book, "Exploring Secrets of the Heavenly Realm." In Galatians 5:1 (NASB) we read:

> *It was for freedom that Christ set us free;*
> *therefore keep standing firm and do not*
> *be subject again to a yoke of slavery.*

Notice again, Paul talking about the about passing under the yoke or harnessing the beast. To the Galatians, the warning was, don't come under the yoke of Judaism. Today, don't fall under the yoke of being religious. The self righteousness through programs and following a set of rules. Living Christianity without the power of the Holy Spirit. Paul says this is a free will choice!

To be honest, I would rather minister to a bunch of sinners than minister to self-righteous or religious people, who have not given themselves over to the Holy Spirit for sanctification. For anyone who desires to follow a set of do's and don'ts for righteousness has fallen under the ache of an evil fallen angel of religion unto demonization.

Moving forward on our topic of wrestling with evil properly, we see that God created the heavens and the earth, then He separated them with an arch of the sky and divided the waters. On earth God placed every creature, including demons who roam the earth, under man's authority of rule. We also know there are no demonic forces who have high enough rank to operate in the second heaven. What the Bible teaches is that fallen angels operate out of the four dimensions and sub-realms of the second heaven and seek to control how earth functions. This happens through a series of processes seeking to establish a system in which mankind works for them through sin. This is plainly visible as human culture sets up laws to manage or run the earth as a business if you will. From the CEO to the mail clerk! This gives the fallen angels the right to conduct military activities in a specific area of human culture to form a base or a stronghold. Let me give you an example of a second heaven fallen angel stronghold or military base in America, abortion. Humanity knows it is wrong! How? By the desire to start a family. But because of human law, the second heaven fallen angels are empowered through ungodly law, and so work through mankind's mind. This process gives demonic spirits rights who work for the fallen, permission to possess, and influence mankind to act to fulfill demonic function. Those functions when multiplied through each human, fulfills the fallen angels desire, and gives them the right to control the course of this evil age.

I've said this in my first book, and I'll say it again here, demonic spirits are individual problems for each human, but fallen angels are cultural and world problems. Activities of mankind reveal the authority and power of fallen angels within each zip code, city, county, region, state, country, continent, globe, and the universe. Demons seek too personally posses individual's through implicit or explicit sin. Demons also seek to posses families, and throughout succeeding generations. The desire of each demon is the power they receive through the coming generations of humanity, who follow in the footsteps of their fathers. Demons want to remain hidden. They accomplish this through engrafting themselves in human personality. The things we like of this world or the things we do in this world.

The bible instructs us to seek sanctification. Not only are we to turn away (repent) from evil, but we are to be set apart to God. We are to obey and follow a lifestyle that is befitting of a believer. Sanctification is to pursue freedom from sin. This will include deliverance and then exorcism. These two words are use simultaneously within Christian circles, but operate on or within different realms. Deliverance is the action Jesus takes of setting a believer free. The believer decrees a formal or authoritative utterance concerning legal rights, alter personalities, curses, strongholds, oaths, vows, ceremonies and the rituals with words within the ceremonies. In today's Church, we call this non-confrontational deliverance. In non-confrontational deliverance the believer is set free by what has been renounced and expelled by some form of wind; wind is the definition of spirit. In non-confrontational deliverance, not all evil will leave. Non-confrontational deliverance is to expel the weaker demons.

Just the word exorcism seems to point to its own definition. The Enhanced Strong's Lexicon defines it as to expel. Expel means to drive out or eject as stated above. It has the implication or suggestion of a violent expulsion, especially of demons. It also states the demon is to come forth from its place. In exorcism, this means to confront the demon. This is a forceful expulsion, where the demon fights in the mind and body of the host, against the deliverance minister. Trying to expose any weakness in his or her's ability and training to cast out. This was clearly brought forth in the examples above and the word wrestle. Remember the word wrestle is from the old Greek "pale," meaning a struggling, wrestling, or hand-to-hand combat. The end result is to forcefully drive out the demons and his subordinates from the places within the human soul and body which they consider their palace. What I mean is that legal rights, curses, strongholds, oaths and vows made all the way back to Adam must be dealt with in these two manners, this is biblical instruction. To have the person seeking deliverance renounce legal rights and curses. Then move to confrontational ministry and bring the demons forth to renounce legal rights, curses, and covenants. This is how we wrestle properly with demonic spirits.

To wrestle properly with fallen angels, we can only look to Jesus with direct combat experience. Jesus is the only one who disarmed fallen angels positionally now and conditionally in the age to come. This is hard for most believers to understand! But simple, if we ask ourselves, is Satan and evil allowed to operate in this evil age of sin? Our answer should be "yes." God's Kingdom is now, but the fulness of God's reign is in the age to come. Where God's reign is, today, there is the Kingdom of God. I will say it this way, God's reign is where His power manifests, both in the future and in the present. This present power of God, is His blessings being poured out through His reign. The opposite then is where the rule of fallen angels exercise their authority and power to rule and reign. Jesus clearly teaches in Matthew 12 and Luke 11, that there are two Kingdoms co-existing. One ruling through righteousness and the other ruling through sin. This is why we can have a miracle and deliverance ministry right next door to a liquor store or an adult movie store. So until we move beyond history, fallen angels in the heavenly realms will stay enthroned where sin dwells.

Kingdom Mandate

The Churches job is to bring heaven to earth, the age to come into this present evil age. The Kingdom of God is entered as believers acknowledge God's will, and from that will enjoy His presence and blessings. The New Testament in general overview, is clear that God's will is not to be fully realized in this age. But we also must acknowledge that through the coming of Christ Jesus the will and reign of God's Kingdom has come in full.

The believers who are willing to deliver people from the powers of darkness, and bring them into the inheritance of the saints in the kingdom of light, weaken the evil spirits within many realms. Once the person becomes born again, then we must expel so that the inheritance is experienced and exercised. Those believers who don't see the need to operate in the power of the Holy Spirit are held captive by fallen angels in their minds. Evil holds gifts, talents, blessings, health, and destinies hostage, and every believer must be exorcised to experience the fulness of those blessings. God said in Colossians 1:18, that Jesus is the head of the Church. The Churches reign in this evil age is in Christ Jesus. Redemption is now, the fulness of our redemption is when the reign of God is experienced at history's end. Paul does encourage us to fulness, not that Paul attained, but he pressed on for which Christ Jesus laid hold of him, the fulness found in Christ Jesus.

Just as there are two appearing's of Christ, the incarnation and the return or second coming of Christ, so there are two manifestations of God's Kingdom. At Jesus' coming, the Kingdom in power of glory. In this present evil age, God's reign is establish as we fulfill Jesus' commission with the gospel He preached. Jesus preached and Paul confirmed, the Kingdom of God is not in word but in power. We are to take the Word of God, His will, and establish God's rule through power encounters. Then, after the millennium when Jesus hands over to the Father all thing under His feet.

Believers have a mandate to engage in spiritual warfare and to see the kingdom of God advance. We must stand, which means to take a strong defensive position, and engage with the Lord's mighty power. This aggressive combat position is to hold to ground taken through righteous living. The believer going through deliverance is to endure through a season or long term, and even large scale if need be, war for their freedom. To be assured of victory in spiritual warfare we must look at Colossians:

> *When you were dead in your transgressions and the uncircumcision of your flesh, He made you alive together with Him, having forgiven us all our transgressions, 14 having canceled out the certificate of debt consisting of decrees against us, which was hostile to us; and He has taken it out of the way, having nailed it to the cross. 15 When He had disarmed the rulers and authorities, He made a public display of them, having triumphed over them through Him. Colossians 2:13-15*

Even through we are dealing with people, we do not wrestle against flesh and blood, but against fallen angels in the celestial realm and demonic spirits in the terrestrial realm. It is the goal of every believer to understand the war is over the mind. Because of sin, the mind of humanity (saved/unsaved) has become captured. This is demonstrated through humanities actions. We see through human action that evil spirits set up, establish, and fortify strongholds. It is the work of evil to keep mankind from grasping these facts. One of the weapons believers have is understanding. Understanding then can lead to proper action, demolishing strongholds.

To clear up a point mentioned a few pages ago, Christ has already defeated Satan, the fallen angels, and demonic spirits. But God is implementing this victory in three stages. The cross was the place where total defeat of evil took place, and put in order the first stage, the believer in Christ exercising that defeat through Jesus' life. The believer living from the life of Christ exercising the authority in that life.

The kingdom of darkness desires to control believers and non-believers through the uncircumcised sinful nature, bring them into captivity, making them slaves of sin. Moses told the Israelites to circumcise their hearts in Deuteronomy 10:16. This means mankind must submit their hearts and their bodies to God's will. Jeremiah 4:4 also makes a similar demand of a circumcised heart. Jeremiah states that if we don't say yes to righteousness and no to evil, God's wrath would go forth like fire and burn up our lives with nothing to quench that judgment. He says it is because our deeds are evil. Paul the Apostle says in Romans 2:29, true circumcision is not a cutting of the body but a change of heart produced by God's Spirit.

Transgression is what a person has done in transgressing the will and law of God by some false step or failure. Meaning that we've crossed spiritual boundaries and step into evil territory, giving evil legal rights for possession under God's judgment against us. The believer is judged according to the sinful nature. Jesus cancelled the certificate of debt through His death on the cross. This certificate belongs to the fallen angels and it is a record of debt. The debt is record of all the laws and statutes we have broken, and our generational line, all the way back to Adam. These are legal documents attesting to the lawlessness of our bloodline in the evil age. They are record events and the facts of those events throughout history.

As concerning lower fallen angels who desire control of the family line, iniquity in the blood lines is their right to control. Higher level fallen angels, it is the iniquity of cities, people groups, territories, countries, nations, continents, and the world. We must take these notes of indebtedness, written down by the fallen angels own hand as proof of obligation. These acts have set families, people groups, and nations on certain courses of action that have brought moral and legal binding agreements between mankind and the fallen angels. There is only one course of action that I know about in breaking these legal documents, the court-room of God through a trial. Where the fallen accuse, and the believer states scripture that refutes and proves wrong these claims through the redemptive work of Christ Jesus. The believer is positionally set free through the cross of Christ. This is our argument in God's court. The argument of the fallen angels in God's court, mankind loves his sinful nature or condition and is willfully desiring to live in it.

CHAPTER FOUR

THE OLD MAN

ORIGIN AND NATURE

The reader may ask why these chapters on the old man and the new man in the book's middle. I have found two things that fallen angels are concerned about, one, how the body of Christ unities under Christ Jesus, and two, the development and growth of the believer as he transforms into the image and likeness of Christ Jesus.

I would like to start this chapter off by making a powerful statement about two persons in the New Testament that have a position of unique importance. This statement is the key to coming to the correct understanding, I could even say, a total revelation of the New Testament. The truth is that we can never properly comprehend the message of the New Testament until we really come to the revelation of these two persons. It is of theological and of supernatural importance that we completely understand their origin, nature, and their destiny. This will help us correctly divide the word of truth with the possibility of maturity if factually administered. It will also help us understand ourselves as we proceed through the sanctification process. Paul the Apostle never gives them a name, but gives them a title. Are you ready for it, they are the old man and the new man. Some entitle them the old self and the new self. I will use both titles in this chapter.

Again we can never really understand the message of the New Testament until we come to the true reality of these two persons, the old self and the new self. I would also say, that most in the body of Christ have not understood these two persons, and do not live a victorious life in Christ Jesus. So let us look at Ephesians 4:20-24:

> *But you did not learn Christ in this way! If in fact you have [really] heard Him and have been taught by Him, just as truth is in Jesus [revealed in His life and personified in Him], that, regarding your previous way of life, you put off your old self [completely discard your former nature], which is being corrupted through deceitful desires, and be continually renewed in the spirit of your mind [having a fresh, untarnished mental and spiritual attitude], and put on the new self [the regenerated and renewed nature], created in God's image, [godlike] in the righteousness and holiness of the truth [liv-*

*ing in a way that expresses to God your gratitude
for your salvation]. Ephesians 4:20-24 AMP*

Paul distinguishes between both natures within the believer. He points out it is the choice of the individual to which nature, the old self or the new self, one would yield too. In verse 17 Paul states we should no longer walk as the Gentiles. The implication is that we as believers could live as Gentiles or unbelievers as a Christian. The word "Walk" means to make one's way or progress. It refers to the choice in how someone would regulate one's life. The decisions one would make as opportunities became clear. Paul is saying, as we live our lives, a certain behavior would come forward that could bring about continued actions that would resemble an unbeliever. In verse 17 Paul is talking about the unbeliever, but by the time he gets down to verse 22, Paul reveals his point. He is saying, the believer has a nature that would show itself as deceitful, lustful, corrupted, just as the unbeliever. This old self as Paul names, would definitely try to influence the believers conduct while alive in the body during this evil age.

Paul is writing to committed Christians and instructing them to no longer live as ungodly people do. He says, and even insists that Christians are to abandon all parts of their former life, and live for the glory of Christ Jesus. Paul sees himself as with or in Christ and is instructing for Christ Himself. The Bible is directing us to no longer order or have arranged our behavior as the unbelievers do from their futile mindset. For the believer to have parts of their mind worldly, is to have a mindset that is useless or empty.

Therefore, so many people, believers and non-believers, experience a lifestyle that brings no satisfaction, because they set their minds on the wrong things and emptiness is all they have.

Paul tells the Ephesians that there is a good possibility they have not heard the truth and or understood their position in Jesus. This is a fact today! Many Christians are so deceived about their position in Christ and their condition according to the old man. Believers quickly want to say, the old man was crucified in Christ, but moments later go out and sin. Believers also want to say on the cross Jesus became a curse for us, but moments later will sin, revealing the curse in their members. Positionally, our old self was crucified on Jesus' cross, in Christ, but what Paul is revealing, the fulfillment of His work on the cross will come at the end of this evil age. Until the return of Christ, Christians will have two natures! Therefore, Paul says to lay aside or to put away, put off our old self. To cease doing what is customary from the old life. We are to remove everything that brings corruption through sin. This is a choice! We are to stop yielding to that which Jesus killed on the cross, the sin nature.

Peter also distinguishes between the old man and the new man when he writes in 1 Peter 1:14 AMP, "[Live] as obedient children [of God]; do not be conformed to the evil desires which governed you in your ignorance [before you knew the requirements and transforming power of the good news regarding salvation]." Again, the implication is the believer could be governed or we could say controlled by the old man. Within this old nature Peter says it is possible for the believer to house evil desires. This old nature the Bible calls the old self has its origin in the Satanic principle.

When we read our scripture again, we see the old self and the new self. As Christians, we are instructed to take specific action regarding these two selves. We are to put off the old self and put on the new self. I like to think of it as getting dressed. It takes time and thought to what I will wear and then to get dressed. The same with getting undressed, it takes time to undress and where I'm putting the dirty clothes. Theology calls this sanctification. Like getting dressed and undressed, it takes time and knowledge for us to go through the sanctification process. If we are to do this, we must understand what it involves. So first, identification of the old self and the new self is a must, otherwise how do we know if we are doing what scripture commands, the putting off or the putting on the two selves. What I'm saying is that scriptural knowledge is essential to the success of this process.

Let us now talk about the origin and nature of the old self. This is a reality that quite a few believers refuse to believe, yet it affects their decision making, the words they speak, and their actions in everyday life. Paul reveals in verse 22 of Ephesians 4, three key thoughts. Paul says the old man is corrupt, it lusts, and is deceitful. What is the meaning of deceit? It means to cheat, deceive, and beguile. From the old self we act dishonestly and treat ourselves and others unfairly. The old self likes to take advantage of others and situations, to benefit themselves. The old self wants to defraud the new self of everything that has been given in Christ Jesus. To defraud, Vine's defines it as to be robbed through the corrupt condition of the mind. The informal meaning of cheating is to be sexually unfaithful. This is an act or product of the old self, to be sexually immoral. Paul tells the Thessalonians in 2 Thess.2:10 that all deceit reveals itself through unrighteousness. Therefore, nothing good comes from the old man. The old man is deceitful and in so being, all manner of unscrupulous words and deeds come forth. From deception, sin came forth! Hebrews 3:13 AMP says, "But continually encourage one another every day, as long as it is called "Today" [and there is an opportunity], so that none of you will be hardened [into settled rebellion] by the deceitfulness of sin [its cleverness, delusive glamour, and sophistication]."Because of the fall of Adam, in this evil age sin will have a pull on us as the writer of Hebrews describes.

Paul says in Romans 16:18 false teachers and their teachings can seduce believers. This happens as these smooth talkers speak what people want to hear, and not the truth. This teaching is like flattery and deceives the minds of naïve people. Anyone who does not believe Paul, Peter, and James has fallen from truth. The old self is programmed from the lie, and through hollow and deceptive doctrine, lead believers into captivity. Peter says these false teachers and doctrines, mouth emptiness (deceit) through boastful words and appealing to the lustful desires of the old self, they entice people to live in error (2 Pet 2:18). New Testament writers continued to teach to be watchful of being led astray by the sinful desires of the old man. The old man then is a seductive force that works against God's saving grace and the inheritance believers are to have in this age and the age to come. James, like Paul, speaks of the deceitful desires of the old self by using imagery of sexual seduction to show how our desires gradually, in subtle ways, bring about harmful effects. These insidious desires of the old self pull us in the wrong direction. James 1:14-15 of the NIV says, "Each one is tempted when, by his own evil desire, he is dragged away and enticed. Then, after desire has conceived, it gives birth to sin; and sin, when it is full-grown, gives birth to death. James spells it out for believers, the twelve tribes or the Christians Jews he was writing too.

The origin of the old self is deception! The old self is the product of deceit or deception. Deception's origin is in Satan. The old self resulted from heeding Satan's lie. Therefore, mankind is so responsive to lies, it pulls its strength from the old self.

In reading Ephesians, much of the imagery is about the Church. We could say, the imagery of the old self and new self is much like the archetypal (a certain kind of person) pattern of the old Adam and the new Adam or the old humanity and the new humanity. One nature takes its pattern after deceit, lusts, and corruption, the other after truth, righteousness, and holiness.

James, Peter and John identify the old man with the world and people at enmity with, those who oppose God's will and purpose. We must come into an understanding it is the fruit of the Spirit of God that produces God's work in us. The word "work" in Galatians 5:19 means toil as an effort and occupation. It has the implication of an act or deeds, meaning to labor in a business. In the gospel of Mark 1:24 the demon says, "what business do we have with each other, Jesus of Nazareth?" The conversation was about a place of employment. The demons job was to bring about the works of the flesh for entry. If we continue to be undisciplined and self-indulgent, the Holy Spirit will not aid in the sanctification process and doors of entry open to evil. Our carnal nature is like an enemy living inside us. It wants what it wants, and Paul says the only way for the old self not to deceive us is to crucify it.

Paul was not an immature Christian when he wrote Romans 7! Paul acknowledges that the old self will be with him during his life in this evil age. He says the old self has nothing good within its nature. We can not expect any good to come out of it. Even if we were to crucify the old man completely, it would be still with us, just not alive. We sees this truth in death! Paul said when the law of God came, he died. The law of God revealed the works of the old man. In Romans 7:1 (AMP) Paul says, "Or do you not know, brothers and sisters (for I am speaking to those who know the Law), that the Law has jurisdiction [to rule] over a person as long as he lives?" Paul is speaking about the old self. Therefore, as long as the sinful nature is working in the believer, the law is condemning that person.

As stated before, the product of the old self is deception, and everything that deceives has its origin in Satan. Adam and Eve found this to be true. Genesis 3:1 uses the word cunning or crafty, speaking of the serpent, Satan. The primary root in the Hebrew is to defraud through acts of treachery. Treachery is an act of betrayal of trust. It is a deceptive action within a nature. Satan, the leader of the fallen angels, got Adam and Eve to betray their trust of faith in God for false information or the lie. The Hebrew word also defines it as to deceive.

The nature of Satan was to conspire against God and he fell for doing it. Adam and Eve listened to Satan, and in so doing conspired within, the product was to beguile or to be charmed, that is to be enticed or lured to obey Satan. Once they did, they came under a new government and fatherhood. Mankind's father would now be Satan and the government would be sin. Man would live in this lifetime in an age where evil rules.

There is another translation of the Hebrew word cunning, it is wiles. Paul warns us in Ephesians 6:11 that we must watch out for the devil's schemes or wiles. Notice the armor of God is for the fallen angels and not the demons. Satan is a metaphor for the fallen. Authority in Christ Jesus is to handle the demonic realm in the earth. But with the fallen angels, we are to know of their strategies.

From the beginning creation has had its origin in God's Word, God said and it came to be. In Genesis 2:17 God said, you are free to eat from any tree in the garden, but you must not eat from the tree of the knowledge of good and evil, [now notice this] when [a timing word] you eat of it you will [curse for disobedience] surely die. Now in Genesis 3:4, Satan said you will not surely die. The temptation was to ignore God's warning, and to disobey what God had told them. The lie was the direct negation or contradiction of what God had said. The belief and act of the direct lie, gave birth to the old self.

From the start of this Chapter, I have been driving to one main point, Satan, and the fallen angels primary weapon against the human race is deception. Through deception comes the ability to possess. In Revelation 12:9, the Bible says, Satan and his angels lead the entire world astray. The word astray means to deceive. To lead away from the right way or truth. The fallen, this includes Satan, seduces the world and causes humanity to wander away from the truth. The Bible pictures Satan and the fallen angels as snakes. A snake will never be straight, but crooked! So the product of the lie is as crooked as the snake himself. This is the old self, crooked like Satan. Jesus says Satan has been lying from the beginning. The lie is the father of the old self, just as truth (Jesus) is the father of the new self.

Deception sets in motion a process of degeneration. Deception produces lust, and lust is perverted rebellious desires. They are desires opposite in nature to the will of God. They are also opposed to the wellbeing of the one who entertains and acts on those lusts. Lust also has a fruit, sin, and sin produces death.

CHAPTER FOUR

THE NATURE OF THE OLD SELF

There is a nature produced by deception and lust. The key word which describes it is corrupt. The nature of the old self is corrupt. This means it is also corruptible. This speaks to a moral decay going through a process for final ruin. The old nature, which is with us until we go to heaven or Jesus comes back, desires to go through a series of actions or steps to achieve a particular end, death. The old self wants to seem natural, causing an involuntary series of changes that bring about sin. The nature of the old man is to destroy through corruption and so bringing into a worse state.

The old self is the offspring of Satan. This reality is found in Genesis 3:15 (AMP),

> *"And I will put enmity (open hostility)*
> *Between you and the woman,*
> *And between your seed (offspring) and her Seed;*
> *He shall [fatally] bruise your head,*
> *And you shall [only] bruise His heel."*

The Lord spoke to the serpent concerning his seed. Because the old self is the offspring or the seed of Satan, it reproduces the nature of Satan. This means the old self has the basic or the inherent features of sin, in so, demonstrating the satanic characteristics. Jesus says in John 8:44, to the religious leaders of His day, "you belong to your father, the devil." We could say then, the devil is a father to the children of disobedience. Where disobedience is in our lives, there is the satanic principal at work. Let me say it this way, it is a person, a demonic spirit or fallen angel, causing us to live and act as their agent or representative. The nature of the spirit being is reproduced in those who are disobedient. This is how a Christian can have a demon. We can easily discern if this is the case by the word rebellion. When we act in disobedience to the Word of God or resist the move of the Holy Spirit, it is revealed within any person, a demonic spirit is at work. The behavior of the old nature is rebellious in its nature.

The function of the old self is to lead the believer away from holiness. Instead of the believer seeking purity, the old man's desire is to defile. When that happens, open doors for evil spirits take place for entry. The old man is ceremonially unholy to God. The flesh of mankind has taken on the nature of Satan and it is defiled. One definition is to dye with another color or staining of a glass. Sin has polluted the old self through moral and physical defilement, it has been blemished. Isaiah 53:6 (AMP) says,

> *All of us like sheep have gone astray,*
> *We have turned, each one, to his own way;*
> *But the Lord has caused the wickedness of us all*
> *[our sin, our injustice, our wrongdoing]*
> *To fall on Him [instead of us].*

The old man caused us to wander from a proper belief or a course of action. To be lead astray or error through the seduction of sin. The mark of the old man in its behavior is to turn to its own way. Isaiah says the old self turns its back on God, seeks its own will, its pleasure and satisfaction without reference to God. It takes no action or suggestions toward God. Paul in Romans 3:10 says, "there is none righteous" or not one who meets God's standard. We see this described in greater detail in Ephesians 2:1-3 (NKJV),

> *And you He made alive, who were dead in trespasses and sins, in which you once walked according to the course of this world, according to the prince of the power of the air, the spirit who now works in the sons of disobedience, among whom also we all once conducted ourselves in the lusts of our flesh, fulfilling the desires of the flesh and of the mind, and were by nature children of wrath, just as the others.*

Colossians 2:13 says we were dead in our transgressions and the uncircumcision of our flesh or in 1:21, alienated and hostile in mind, engaged in evil deeds. King David said in Psalm 51:5, he was brought forth in iniquity, and in sin his mother conceived him. We see in Ephesians that the product of the lie is the sons of disobedience. Paul says the old nature wants to live according to the course of this world, the way it operates through its beliefs. This passage of scripture is a description of those who still have the old self. Paul says, Satan, and the fallen angels can work in them, believer or non-believer, because of disobedience. Satan can work in, that is the key, to work in through rebellion. The old self is borne a rebel and there lies the satanic principle.

Paul says, we all once conducted ourselves in the lusts of our flesh. Notice the free will to obey these lusts. These lust are regarding those evil desires which are ready to express themselves in bodily activity. They are seated in the emotions of the soul and or the natural tendencies toward evil things. We could say, they are passions that exist in the soul and emotions that desire to express themselves in activities.

Notice Paul says the old man wants to fulfill the desires or lusts of the flesh and of the mind. The satanic principle works through the unrenewed mind, an established a stronghold in our emotions, working or producing through sinful acts. Remember, we said the satanic principle is a foundation and system of beliefs that cause behavior by a chain of reasonings, all based on lies.

We all notice people with beliefs, behavior and attitudes that line up with the course of this evil age. The person's behavior is manifest in several applications that vary according to its yielding to the old man who's father is Satan. By nature we are sons of disobedience and disobedience always bring about God's wrath. Here is Paul's meaning throughout his epistles to the Church, there is a rebel living inside each one of us believers. Recapping, Satan's deception produces lust, lust produces sin, sin produces death. The nature of the old self produced in this way has two distinctive marks, first it is corrupt spiritually, morally, physically, and secondly it is a rebel.

CHAPTER FOUR

GOD'S SOLUTION FOR THE OLD SELF

If understanding is to come to us through the New Testament, the mystery of the old self and the new self is of vital importance. So much doctrinal error has come forth from this mystery. Bible mysteries are things that have been hidden in the past, but now are to be produced through the light. The old self is a problem that confronts everyone of us. It is a theological understanding that presents itself to all humanity. It cannot be explained away or covered by some error of interpretation or a blanket scripture. When we miss diagnose ourselves through scriptural error, it brings us into the realm of arguments or face-to-face hostility with others and even ourselves. The entire human race, as long as we live in this evil age, the old self plagues the whole human race. Why? We in the flesh have all descended from Adam. This is the disease that has come to humanity, sin.

For us to understand God's solution, we must rule out certain methods that are not scriptural, but seem to be ingrained deep within the Church. Churches aid and help through self realization, teaching in someone's potential outside of the leadings and promptings of the Holy Spirit for sanctification. Telling believers to do it yourself by character, coming from a position in scripture. Leaving the believer to act in the flesh on falsely fulfilling they're own righteousness. This leads to what I call self fulfillment and the believer trying to achieve by striving for scriptural hopes and ambitions without the empowering work of the Holy Spirit. Here's another issue in the Church, self expression. Everyone has their own thoughts and feelings, which depend on their own desires, scriptural or not. Let me give you an example. The Bible clearly states we shall not tattoo, yet believers have their own person self expression. Have you noticed the word "self." Christians will say, well that is old covenant, yet Paul the Apostles says, I would not have known what sin was unless the law revealed it. Sin has its origin in the satanic nature, this is Bible doctrine 101. Self-expression can be stated as one who works out their own salvation. All these things give freedom to the old self which is a rebel in God's view. All solutions which have there foundation in self are giving free reign to a rebellious nature.

We also see within the Church, a system of law. Believers turning to the law to deal with the old self. Here is one that may sting, the works of the Holy Spirit were for the Apostles and they passed away after they established the early Church. We describe this belief in one word, legalism. Israel's failure is proof that to live by a set of laws does not achieve God's desired end. Paul in Romans 7 states that the law is holy, righteous, and good. So there is nothing wrong with law, but law can not change the rebel. The law actually disapproves of the rebel and condemns him to death. Therefore, we don't tattoo. Why did I pick tattooing as my example, because it brings out those self expressions, self realizations, and self fulfillments?

Religion does not change the rebel. God did not design the old self to go to Church, attend self-help groups, memorize scripture, or be a part of a cell group for transformation. These things in their self are good, but it will not alter or transform the old self. Derek Prince says in his teaching somewhere within the old self and new self mp3, that religion is like a refrigerator, it can temporarily hide corruption, but it cannot ultimately change it. Somewhere in his teaching he says, and these are not quotes, religion is like a piece of fruit, looks good, ripe and appetizing. Yet left in the refrigerator, it will ultimately rot. Why? The process of corruption is already at work within the fruit. We can incarcerate or slow down that process of corruption by refrigeration. But because of corruption, that piece of fruit that grew on that vine or tree, was birthed to die if not eaten. Quite a few Christian lives remind me of this process. Going to Church, yet not taking advantage of crucifying the old self. The Church can incarcerate religion, or conceal it, but it in the end cannot change it. Self realization, the law, and religion cannot change the old self.

> *So every good tree bears good fruit, but the bad tree bears bad fruit. A good tree cannot produce bad fruit, nor can a bad tree produce good fruit. Every tree that does not bear good fruit is cut down and thrown into the fire. So then, you will know them by their fruits. Matthew 7:17-20 NASB*

Jesus is using a tree as an example of the two selves, the fallen part of man, and the future regeneration or the born again man. Paul has labelled them as the old self and the new self. The old self cannot produce good fruit, and so the new self cannot produce bad fruit. The old self or that tree must be cut down. What was Jesus referring to, in New Testament language, He was referring to crucifixion?

The old self must be done away with. There is no remedy for the old self outside of crucifixion. The good news of the gospel tells us that execution has already taken place in Christ. This is what theology calls, positional Christianity. As I opened this chapter, this is the key to understanding the gospel message. The key is positional verses conditional Christianity. We must take our condition in this present evil age in the old self off and put it to death. We must put on our new self which is created in Christ Jesus and I must now live according to the leadings and promoting's of the Holy Spirit, in so not fulfilling the desires of the flesh. Let's look at how the living bible describes these two selves in Romans 7:21-25:

It seems to be a fact of life that when I want to do what is right, I inevitably do what is wrong. 22 I love to do God's will so far as my new nature is concerned; 23-25 but there is something else deep within me, in my lower nature, that is at war with my mind and wins the fight and makes me a slave to the sin that is still within me. In my mind I want to be God's willing servant, but instead I find myself still enslaved to sin.

So you see how it is: my new life tells me to do right, but the old nature that is still inside me loves to sin. Oh, what a terrible predicament I'm in! Who will free me from my slavery to this deadly lower nature? Thank God! It has been done by Jesus Christ our Lord. He has set me free.

Paul is an Apostle, he is born again, in-filled with the Holy Spirit, a worker of miracles, healings, and deliverances. Most scholars agree that Romans was written around A.D. 56. It was about 8 years later that Paul was put to death. Paul had not attained perfection and is writing about what must take place inside the believer. He is writing about the key or secret of the success of the believer.

Let us examine this text and insert ourselves within. When we want to do right or have a will to do good, do we find another law at work or do we inevitably do wrong? An honest answer is yes! Paul says when we are doing God's will and loving it, causing delight within, that comes from the inward man or the new nature. The Apostle says he recognizes another spiritual law within his members, something else deep within him, this lower nature. Paul finds these two natures are at war within the mind, bringing him into captivity to the law of sin which he finds in the lower nature, the old self. The old self wins the fight and Paul becomes a slave to sin that is still within the lower nature or old self.

Throughout Paul's journey as a Christian, he speaks here about the power of the believer through the secret of the two natures. Paul says, in my mind I want to be God's willing servant, but instead I find myself still enslaved to sin.

So you see how it is: my new life tells me to do right, but the old nature is still inside me loves to sin. He needs deliverance from the old self and says, who will free me from my slavery to this deadly lower nature? Thank God! It has been done by Jesus Christ our Lord. He has set me free. Paul's amazing answer is that it was already done in Christ

Jesus positionally. We have the victory in Christ and the power through the Holy Spirit to crucify the old self. Notice how the New King James closes chapter 7, "So then, with the mind I serve the law of God, but with the flesh the law of sin." Romans 8 shows us how the new self is supposed to thrive.

Let us look at Romans 6:6-8 on how Jesus has set us free.

We know that our old sinful selves were crucified with Christ so that sin might lose its power in our lives. We are no longer slaves to sin. For when we died with Christ we were set free from the power of sin. And since we died with Christ, we know we will also live with him. Romans 6:6-8 NLT

I have found that most Christians don't know the truth about the old self and the new self. First, Paul reveals positional Christianity by stating that those who are born again were crucified with Christ. They also call this substitutional Christianity. Jesus died in my place, so I'm to believe and no longer live for myself. When Paul states that we might do away the body of sin that is conditional Christianity. Might is a word that expresses possibility! It means there is a sanctification process we are to invoke. Paul says as we go through sanctification, sin loses its power. Positionally we have the new self, which is free from sins power and not enslaved to sin. Verse 7 states he who has died, died to what, the old self. We believe we shall (present/future) live with Him. So, the only way of escape from the slavery of sin, to crucify the old lower nature called the old man.

Because of Jesus, we don't have to be enslaved by the lower nature. I will not argue concerning the two selves, only the Holy Spirit can give insight and revelation on the subject of these two natures. Our old self is the criminal. In closing the chapter, God's solution for the old man is execution, so that the power of sin will no longer bring the believer into captivity, but freedom through the born again new man that the Holy Spirit regenerated by right of Jesus' crucifixion, burial, resurrection, and ascension or glorification.

Recapping, the old self is the product of deception, that is, of Satan's lie. That which denies the truth of God's Word. Deception then gave birth to lust, perverted damaging desires. When lust is yielded too, produces sin, and sin when it takes its course produces death. This is the scriptural degenerative process of the old man. The old man has two distinctive characteristics, first, it is corrupt (spiritually, morally, and physical), and secondly it is a rebel.

CHAPTER FIVE

THE NEW MAN

In our last chapter, I dealt with the origin and nature of the old self. We concluded that the old self is the product of deception, that is, of Satan's lie. That which denies the truth of God's Word. Deception then gave birth to lust, perverted damaging desires. When lust is yield too, produces sin, and sin when it takes its course produces death. This is the scriptural degenerative process of the old man. The old man has two distinctive characteristics, first, it is corrupt (spiritually, morally, and physically), and secondly it is a rebel. So, the old self responds to deception, the product of a lie. Deception is the action, through a lie, that deceives or causes us to believe a lie. Deception produces evil lusts that causes sin which leads to death. Let us look at our scripture from Ephesians:

That you put off, concerning your former conduct, the old man which grows corrupt according to the deceitful lusts, 23 and be renewed in the spirit of your mind, 24 and that you put on the new man which was created according to God, in true right- eousness and holiness. Ephesians 4:22-24 NKJV

In this chapter I will explain the nature and origin of the new man. Again from our scripture, we can plainly see our old self and our new self. This is something that cannot be argued or theologically explained away. This is sound bible doctrine or as the definition states, a set of beliefs held to and taught by scripture. Those that deny the lower nature inside, have fallen into deception.

We see from our scripture four main aspects of the new man. First it is produced from a creative act of God, the born again creation. This is something humanity cannot do on its own. Jesus in John 3 says, Spirit (Holy Spirit) gives birth to spirit (human spirit). Any act of man cannot produce the creative regeneration of the human spirit. Religion fails, as does good works or legalism, the new man is a creative act of God. This creative act of God proceeds out of the truth, only out of the truth of God's Word. This process is the exact opposite which death came through the lie. From our scripture we see there is a nature to produce in the new man, this nature is righteousness and holiness. Paul says, this new man is in the likeness of God. The new man is according to the purpose of God. God's purpose or His reason for which He created the new man is about His likeness. It was God's determination to bring about

His creation for which the new man exists, His original purpose for creating mankind.

The new man is the idea, the thought and suggestion of the original purpose for man. Man was to reflect God's likeness and man was to be God's expression. Jesus being the last Adam, the end of something, has set forth God's likeness in Himself. Jesus is God's expression of God's glory and nature. Jesus, the incarnation, expressed the very thought and feelings of God in words and deeds. It is in Jesus that the new self is restoring the likeness of God throughout the earth.

> *Do not lie to one another, for you have stripped off the old (unregenerate) self with its evil practices, and have clothed yourselves with the new [spiritual self], which is [ever in the process of being] renewed and remolded into [fuller and more perfect knowledge upon] knowledge after the image (the likeness) of Him Who created it. Colossians 3:9-10 AMP*

Paul says lying is the root manifestation or the expression of the old self. All lies have their origin in Satan and in so, is a liar by nature. Paul says, put on the new self who is being renewed to a true and perfect knowledge according to the image or likeness of God who is the creator of the new self.

Colossians states, the new self is being remolded or progressively renewed. When we look back at Ephesians 4, Paul is emphasizing the act of creation, but in Colossians, Paul stresses the process of being renewed. We can conclude from both Ephesians and Colossians the special importance Paul is desiring his readers to focus in on. Not only the creation of the new man, but the process of sanctification of the new man. If we lose focus of these two points Paul is emphasizing, then we can be led astray, and be in doctrinal error.

Sanctifications first meaning is that of being set apart to God. This happens when we become born again, God's creative act of regenerating the human spirit of those who except Christ as Lord and Savior. Sanctification also implies a course of life that is befitting one's salvation, this is the process. The process is of the separation of evil things by the believer. Paul is stating, this is the will of God. Just as the truth of God's Word gave birth, so it is the gospel that calls, and the believer who must learn as it teaches. It is the Apostles directive for the new man to first come back into the true knowledge of God and secondly, Paul uses the image of his creator, the new man reflecting God's likeness. So the new man is being progressively renewed and secondly fulfilling the two end purposes of God, the true knowledge of God and the restoration of God's image or likeness through holiness.

THE NEW MAN MANUFACTURED

What does the Bible say about how the new man is produced? Ephesians 4:24 says his creation is by a birth, created is the operative word. The gospel of John, in chapter 3, verses 3-8, Jesus speaks of being born again. Theology uses the word regeneration. Regeneration is a secret act of God in which He imparts new spiritual life to us. John 1:13 collaborates the statement, "born of God." In the work of regeneration we play no active role, it is totally a work of God. John 1:13 specifically says those who are children of God, are born of God. Ezekiel 36:26-27 references the old man and the new man:

> *I will give you a new heart and put a new spirit in you; I will remove from you your heart of stone and give you a heart of flesh. And I will put my Spirit in you and move you to follow my decrees and be careful to keep my laws. Ezekiel 36:26-27 NIV*

God's sovereign work in regeneration, God promises through the prophetic word of Ezekiel, He would give a new spiritual life to those who accept Christ's work of atonement. It is God working as the third person of the trinity, the Holy Spirit produces regeneration. In 1 Peter 1:23, "For you have been born again, not of perishable seed, but of imperishable, through the living and enduring word of God." From Ezekiel it was the prophetic word and from Peter, it is the written word, yet both have their source in God. When God speaks, the exact relationship in time between regeneration and the proclamation of the gospel is difficult to define, but God is effectively calling man to salvation through His Word. Let me say it this way, when God speaks, He is virtually calling or summoning to Himself a people that receive a new spiritual life through regeneration.

The New Testament is very clear on the spiritual position of the old man and the new man. The old man is dead and produces works of death. But the new man is spiritually alive, is living for God, and producing works of righteousness and holiness. As we receive God's Word by faith and obey it, God's Spirit brings forth within us the very nature of God. As Derek Prince would say somewhere in his teachings, divine, incorruptible, and eternal.

We are talking about how the new man is produced or manufactured. I use the word manufactured because it gives the picture of something that one builds progressively. There is a beginning, and it starts with being born again. This new creation is being built. God design it and through a process of construction, to be a reflection or an image of God, in truth, righteousness, and holiness.

The new self is incorruptible, it is the very nature of God, coming out of the Word of God. That seed of the preached Word of God, or the Living Word of God [Jesus] received and believed, brings forth the nature, and the person of God, Jesus.

> *I have been crucified with Christ; it is no longer I who live, but Christ lives in me; and the life which I now live in the flesh I live by faith in the Son of God, who loved me and gave Himself for me. Galatians 2:20 NKJV*

We can now see the two selves so clear. Paul says God's program for the old self is a crucifixion in Christ, but also an ongoing crucifixion, the life Paul lives in the flesh. To live by faith Paul says is to put the Word of God to work and let it build within, the new man, form the image of God within. We go nowhere until we execute of old self. Our old self was crucified on the cross with Christ and Paul says it is now Christ who is living in him, not living for the old self. We call this positional and conditional Christianity. Positionally my old self was crucified in Christ on the cross, but conditionally my old man is going through a death process. The key to the New Testament is to understand that positionally I live in Christ and have the power to say no to sin through God's grace. As long as we live in this evil age, the sin nature or the old man, will always be a reminder how evil sin really is. It is God's design in this age, that man have a connection with sin, so we can truly see how harmful sin is. Each believer much understand the correct New Testament teaching on justification, sanctification, and glorification.

How To Develop The New Man

Paul says in Ephesians 4:23, there is something we must do. He says we are to be renewed in the spirit of our mind. To put off the old self, there must be a total change in the mind, in the way we think. What Paul is proclaiming is to become a different person entirely, to be transform on the inside into the likeness of Jesus. The old self is a child of the devil, it was produced out of deceit. Deceit or deception activates lusts, and when we act on lusts, these harmful desires, it brings forth death. The new man has the ability in Christ Jesus to alter the agreements the old self has made to evil. The new self has been born of God, a child of God, and through the transformed mind, moves from darkness to light. Paul explains these two selves so powerfully in Romans, chapters 6-8. In the new spiritual birth, sins power was broken over us. Spiritually we became part of Christ Jesus through His death and resurrection. Through Jesus' death the sinful nature was weakened, but not done away with. We could say, it was mortally wounded, powerless if you will to the new man.

We have become one with Christ, we positionally died with Him, and now we positionally share His new life through our born again spirit. Positionally, our old evil desires through the old self was nailed to the cross in Christ, judged, crushed, and fatally wounded. This happened so that our sin loving old self is no longer under sin's control. We who are spiritual know sin is a person, and that person and his kingdom have been sinning from the beginning. The new man no longer needs to be a slave to sin.

For when we allow the new nature control, the new man, we have become deadened to sin's power and control. We have become freed from all its passions that lure or lust, and this is what it means to be free from sin's power over us. Paul reveals, since our old self died with Christ positionally, we know that our new self will share in His life. We see sanctification here. This is what Paul is saying about the renewing of the mind. The renewed mind understands that death no longer has power through the old self because the new self lives a life of unbroken fellowship with God.

The transformation of the mind starts when we look upon our old sinful nature and its passions and desires as dead, no longer pulling on us. We could say, we are now unresponsive to sin. The new self is alive to God, alert and responsive to the Holy Spirit, through our new life in Christ Jesus. The mind of the new self will not allow sin to control the body any longer. It will not give in to sinful desires, and refuse the old self to become instruments or tools of wickedness, glorifying sin's power. The new self desires to yield completely to God. The mind of the new self says, every part of creation, spirit, soul, and body, is obedient to the Spirit of God to use as instruments of righteousness or used for God's purpose.

The new creation [new self] says, sin will never enslave me again through the old self. It says sin will not be my master because I am no longer tied to laws that bring death where sin gaines power. The mind of the new self says, I am free through Christ, empowered over the old self and sin, and completely under the control of the Holy Spirit, experiencing God's favor and mercy. Therefore, the believer can no longer willfully sin. When we willfully chose to sin, we surrender to the old self empowered by sin, and makes us a prisoner to that person, sin, as master. God's grace shown in the new-created man, will not keep on sinning. The transformed mind of the new-created self, says if I can't say no to the person of sin, I will be delivered through Christ. Deliverance is the only option. The new self understands the laws of God and realizes I can give in to the old self and death or I can choose obedience and be acquitted of any guilt.

As one who has done thousands of exorcisms, if we chose obedience to sin, we obey a spiritual person of evil. The Bible says, to the one to whom we offer ourself's, he will take you and become your master. This means we allow through the old self to be enslaved to that evil spirit being.

Through God's creation of the new self, we now obey with our hearts the gospel to which God has committed us. As the new self reigns, conditionally we are being set free from our old self, no longer under his mastery and his power of sin. But through the new self, we have a new master, Christ Jesus, and we reign and rule through righteousness and holiness. Paul is writing this way, using illustrations of slaves and masters because it is easy to picture and so understand. In Christ, we are to be slaves to all that is right and holy, exhibiting and reflecting God's image and likeness.

The mind of the new self, desires exposure or to be exposed to contact with the Holy Spirit. I chose the word exposure, because it means experiencing a condition, identity, or fact. In Romans 12:2, Paul says the new man will learn from exposure how God's ways really are, and through them it will satisfy us. The mind of the new self says look, the behavior and customs of this world or evil age is not to be obeyed. It is the Holy Spirit working through the new self that brings to us the truth. He teaches us how to overcome the old self, and in so doing, defeating the powers of sin, and the evil spirit beings that rule this evil age. To be conformed to this world is to let the old self have his way in our lives. To be transformed, is to yield to the new self who is empowered by the Holy Spirit. The new self is seeking the will of God, which is the development and maturing of the new self. To develop means to go through a process of growth and advancement, being refined into the likeness and image of Christ Jesus. To mature, is to grow up in our salvation. Going through stages of thought, reaching for the most advanced stages of the new self, as our mind is renewed to God's will. We can understand this or take it one step further in Ephesians 1:18,

> *I pray that the eyes of your heart may be enlight-*
> *ened, so that you will know what is the hope of*
> *His calling, what are the riches of the glory of His*
> *inheritance in the saints. Ephesians 1:18 NASB*

We see Paul tell the believer what further needs to happen in this transformation of the mind and the new self. Notice, it is the Holy Spirit who is to flood our hearts with light or truth, so we can see the hope of our calling, the full development of the new self and its destiny. Our development as we advance in our calling or the maturing of the new self, we take part in the future or the power of the age to come, in which we were called to share.

There is a day coming when the new self will fully manifest its self that day will come at the resurrection. Paul says, flesh and blood or the old self, cannot enter the Kingdom of God, 1Cor.15:50. Our bodies must undergo a transformation so they are no longer made up of flesh and blood, but a spiritual body. The old self who has the nature of Satan, made up of flesh and blood, corrupted by sin will die, this is part of the curse. It is also a witness for the believer today, to no longer allow the old self to reign in our mortal bodies.

We know that judgment will terminate this evil age and bring the sons of the Kingdom into their full inheritance of the Kingdom, the completion of the new self. What will happen at the end of this sinful age, Jesus says the angels will come and separate the evil from the righteous? God will glorify those who have chosen to live from the new self and shine like the sun in the Kingdom of God. Those who have lived by the old self have never really known God, they will be thrown into the fiery furnace where there will weep and gnashing of teeth. It is from the new self we come to know God. Paul says our hearts have been in darkness and it is the Holy Spirit who brings our hearts the light of truth.

When Jesus returns at the end of this evil age (Rev.19:11-16) and before the age to come (Rev.21:1) there is an interval when the saints are raised to reign with Christ for a thousand years. This is when the new self will be fully manifested, at the Millennium. The Church age is the period of Christ's invisible glory, when the new self is hidden in a jar of clay. Paul says in Philippians 3 that he had given up everything, dying to the old self, so he could come to know Christ and to experience the mighty power through the new self or as the Living Bible states, brought him back to life again. Paul said he had not been made perfect or the new creation perfected, but he would keep working toward that day when he would finally be all that Christ recreated him to be.

The Millennium will be the period of the manifested glory of Christ and all those who have believed in Him. The glorification of the new self will be a witness of the triumphant Kingdom of God within history, the Millennium. The Millennium is the reign of the visible Christ, so the age to come [eternity] is the reign of the Father. It is scripturally called the age to come. At that time, the age to come, there will be the resurrection of the dead, those who lived governed by the old self, and the destruction of the gods of the evil age.

Revelation 20 speaks of two resurrections, one at the beginning of the Millennium and a second resurrection at the end of the Millennium. We also find stages in the conquest over Satan and the fallen angels. When Jesus returns at the end of this evil age and the Millennium starts, Satan and his angels are thrown into the abyss and chained for a thousand years. You need to follow me very closely here. Jesus' return is the glorification of the new self for those that have believed in Christ in this evil age. At the end of the Millennium, Satan and his fallen angels are released to engage in their wicked, sinful activities again. Some of mankind will survive the tribulation and enter the Millennium, and even though Christ is ruling, the old self within them will respond to evil and the attractions of evil through the old self, and rebel against Christ.

How does that happen, the old self responds to its fathers will? We ask, how powerful is the old man? When the glorified Christ is reigning in glory and power during the Millennium, Satan and the fallen angels will still find hearts of men who have refused salvation and are still responsive to sin through the old self.

Therefore, the Holy Spirit has to bring us the light of truth. It is only through the truth we can see what God has for us in the new self. What we can't forget, and is vital to the growth of the new self, is the Holy Spirit working through the mirror of the Word of God. As we renew our minds, the new self, the new creation operates from the age to come. Today, we have the choice to obey the message of God's Word, not just listen to it. Don't fall prey to the old self, for if we listen and not obey, we are looking into a mirror which reflects the new man, but if we walk away, and forget, we can't see the new man anymore. This is what James is referring too. But, if we steadily look into God's Word, we will remember and do what it says and be transformed into Christ's likeness. God blesses us as the new man is developed. James says, the Word of God is a mirror that is held up before us. The new self is reflected in that mirror, but some will walk away and disregard that likeness, follow after the old man and perish. This is the lukewarm believer! Destined for destruction! Some will look into the law of liberty, freedom from the old self, looking intently, and abide by it, this is the believer who lives in this evil age blessed. So the mirror is revealing what God's grace desires for the new self, freedom!

Now the Lord is the Spirit; and where the Spirit of the Lord is, there is liberty. But we all, with unveiled face, beholding as in a mirror the glory of the Lord, are being transformed into the same

image from glory to glory, just as by the Spir-
it of the Lord. 2 Corinthians 3:17-18 NKJV

Paul says, the Lord is the Spirit, and where God's Spirit is, the new man is, and there is freedom. Through the
new creation, the Lord has removed the veil and we can
see through the new self and reflect the glory of the Lord.
The reflection of God is through the development of the
new self as He transforms us. Notice the transformation
of the new self is into the same image as the Lord, going
from glory to glory, just as the Holy Spirit makes us more
and more like Jesus. We restore the image of God through
the new self, and it is a process of ongoing victory. Notice,
the one who is working this process is the Holy Spirit. Yet
He only works as we are looking into the mirror of God's
Word, desiring obedience.

There is one more important principal we cannot leave
out in our connection of the two selves, and it is this, the
new man grows at the cost of the old man. The new self
tastes and sees that this new life is fulfilling, and says, Jesus must increase and I must decrease. Let us say it this
way, the new man in Christ must increase and the old man
created in the likeness of Satan must decrease. What I am
implying is, only in proportion to the willingness of the
death of my old self, will my new self grow! There has to
be a death if there is going to be a new life. Two key points
here, we must accept what God says about the old man,
and it must be crucified. Positionally, the old man was
crucified with Christ, Romans 6:6, and conditionally, we
must consider ourselves dead to the power of sin, Romans

6:11. These are two facts that must be received by faith since it is the Word of God. Many writers and theologians can't accept these two scriptural facts! Again, the first fact is positionally the old sinful self was crucified and second, conditionally we are not to let sin control the way we live by giving into sins desires. We are not to any part of our body become an instrument of evil to serve sin, Romans 6:12-13. Paul says the old self will want to go on acting as if he has rights. We are not to give in, but to live from the new self which is alive in Christ Jesus. The new self presents himself to the Holy Spirit by yielding our members. What gives the Holy Spirit access, obedience? These are the facts, and this is correct theology. So, we must examine the truth of God's Word and let it reveal the two natures. What we were by nature, the old self, and what we can become by grace, the new self. We must systematically deny the desires of the old self, and yield to the influence of the Holy Spirit. We can express the result with one word in our conduct, obedience.

God's Agenda for the New Self

To understands God's purpose for the new man, we realize that when God arranged a purpose for man, He never gives up on it. So we must start at the beginning. From scripture we learn that sin and Satan may delay God's reason for which man was created, but both can never ultimately thwart it. The new man was created in righteousness, holiness, and truth. The new man's home is the age to come. The new man doesn't belong to this evil age, it doesn't like sin, sickness and suffering. At the coming of

Christ, then the righteous are raised, the new man will experience the fullness of the Kingdom of God. The new self has the ability to receive the blessings of the future age in the present. Christ give Himself for our sins to deliver us from the present evil age. How can mankind who lives in this present evil age be delivered from its power? The deliverance comes through the power of the age come living through the new man.

> For it is impossible [to restore and bring again to repentance] those who have been once for all enlightened, who have consciously tasted the heavenly gift and have become sharers of the Holy Spirit, and have felt how good the Word of God is and the mighty powers of the age and world to come, if they then deviate from the faith and turn away from their allegiance—[it is impossible] to bring them back to repentance, for (because, while, as long as) they nail upon the cross the Son of God afresh [as far as they are concerned] and are holding [Him] up to contempt and shame and public disgrace. Hebrews 6:4-6 AMP

Because of the power of the two natures, those inward characteristics that are graphed in the chemical makeup of the person, the inherited qualities, if at one time a person becomes born again, regenerated, but returns to the world, it is of no use trying to bring them back to the Lord again. The writer to the Hebrews key phrase, and the great divide in the body of Christ's theology, if the person has understood repentance, the power within the new man over sin, experienced the ongoing process of the transformation of the new man, the presence and power of Christ Jesus in them through the Holy Spirit, if they turn back to that indwelt lower nature, the old man, to bring them back to repentance. I've seen true conversions, touches of the Holy Spirit, but thousands have not understood, and turned back because the old man loves the world.

Some school's of thought would like to say, the person who walks away from the Lord was never really saved. These school's of thought will say, once saved, always saved. They quote 1 John 2:19,

They went out from us [seeming at first to be Christians], but they were not really of us [because they were not truly born again and spiritually transformed]; for if they had been of us, they would have remained with us; but they went out [teaching false doctrine], so that it would be clearly shown that none of them are of us. 1 John 2:19 AMP

In balancing these scriptures of Hebrews and John properly, we find the secret in the old man and the new man. Hebrew 6 says they once understood the gospel. This comes in line with 1 John 2 where he says, seeming to be Christians. They tasted of the good things of heaven and the Holy Spirit, even knowing the Word of God. We must stop right here, if someone belongs to the world, they can never taste of the powers of heaven, because they are not born again and belong to the devil. The Bible clearly teaches that a man must be born again to enter or taste of the

Kingdom of God, the power of the age to come. To enter the Kingdom of God, one must be regenerated.

What is John really saying in balance with Jesus and Hebrews? He is saying, that person never allowed the born again experience to impact their life or to take root and grow, much like Matthew 13. 1 John 2:19, this scripture on the surface and if it stood alone, we would have to conclude that the person never really got saved. This is in direct contradict with Jesus' teaching in John 3 about entering the Kingdom through the born again experience. Hebrews even says they have turned against God. You can't turn against God unless you have turned to God.

As we turn back to God's agenda, in Ephesians 1:11, Paul says, because of what Christ has done, we have a destiny, claimed by God as His own, for an inheritance, having been predestined or chosen beforehand according to God purpose in Christ who works everything according to His counsel and design of His will. Everything is coming in line with God's purpose and will. This is in accordance to God's original purpose in creating man. Sin, sickness, even Satan, may have delayed God's plan for man, but cannot stop it. God will ultimately work out His purpose and His plan. This plan is so clearly portrayed in what the New Testament says about the old self and the new self.

In Genesis 1:26-28 reveals what God did in Christ, and so elegantly brought forward in the New Testament. Genesis is talking about mankind, not just one individual man. Let us look at the two main purposes of God in creating humanity. Man is to reflect God's likeness, because man is made in God's image and likeness. God did not rest until He brought forth His likeness in the creation. The second purpose in creating man is to exercise God's authority. If mankind was created in an image, then within that image is authority. Man was to rule over all the earth on God's behalf. Psalm 115:16 confirms man's rule in the interests of God. We find man's authority as he rules as God would rule, exercising God authority over all the earth.

When man sinned, it frustrated both of God's purposes for man. We see that God's image and likeness was spoiled, and man became a slave. Jesus came and restored God's image and likeness by state in John 14:9, if you have seen Me, then you have seen the Father. This is the revelation of the new man, likeness and authority. In John 14:10, Jesus says it is the Father that abides in Him that is doing the work. Jesus is saying the words and works are from the Fathers authority. In John 20:21, so Jesus said to them again, "Peace to you! As the Father has sent Me, I also send you." In the same way the Father sent Jesus and in the victories Jesus attained, so are we to go through the new creation? Jesus came in the authority of the Father, now we through the new man go in that same authority through Christ Jesus. This is so important to understand. Our authority as a believer is in understanding how the Kingdom of God operates, this only comes through the new self.

Jesus came to fulfill the purposes of the Father which Adam through his fall could not do. Sin brought about the old self which was and cannot follow or be successful in fulfilling God's plan for mankind. The new man now can reveal God's likeness again, and to exercise God's authority. Jesus has paved the way for all to do as He did.

> *For those whom He foreknew, He also pre-*
> *destined to become conformed to the image*
> *of His Son, so that He would be the firstborn*
> *among many brethren. Romans 8:29 NASB*

This is a perfect scripture for God's destiny of the new self. Paul is describing God's purpose for the new man and uses the word conformed. It means to make of like form or "to bring to the same form with" some other person or thing, "to render like." The noun morphē refers to the outward expression of an inward essence or nature. Thus, in the process of sanctification, the saint is transformed in his inner heart life to resemble the Lord Jesus. The new self being transformed into the image, likeness, with authority, as he grows in nature of Christ Jesus. Notice it was God's purpose to bring forth many children of Jesus' likeness. In closing the chapter, we are to exercise Christ's authority on His behalf.

> *And Jesus came up and spoke to them, saying,*
> *"All authority has been given to Me in heaven*
> *and on earth. Go therefore and make disciples*
> *of all the nations, baptizing them in the name*
> *of the Father and the Son and the Holy Spir-*
> *it, teaching them to observe all that I commanded*
> *you; and lo, I am with you always, even to the*
> *end of the age." Matthew 28:18-20 NASB*

After Jesus' resurrection, He says, all authority belongs to Him, and He now sends us in the power of the transformed new self. We go on Jesus' behalf to exercise authority with demonstrations of power, as His representatives. Making disciples is expressed as believers teach and model how to execute the old self and release the new self in the power of Christ Jesus. What we teach is the delegated authority of the Lord Jesus Christ.

One last point that is of great importance! The purpose of God in bringing forth many children is to bring a collective body of believers as one new man as stated in Ephesians 2:14-15.

> *For He Himself is our peace, who made both groups into one and broke down the barrier of the dividing wall, by abolishing in His flesh the enmity, which is the Law of commandments contained in ordinances, so that in Himself He might make the two into one new man, thus establishing peace. Ephesians 2:14-15 NASB*

God's overall purpose for the new man is a body of believers operating as one new man. This cannot happen unless the Church turns back to the Holy Spirit. God's design is for the new man to operate through a corporate body, the Church, to bring forth His likeness and authority. Notice Ephesians 4:16, from whom the whole body, being fitted and held together by what every joint supplies, according to the proper working of each individual part, causes the growth of the body for the building up of itself in love.

We are to be one complete corporate body, expressing one new corporate man. This new man is to reenact Christ earthly ministry and fulfills God's two purposes, revealing God to the world and exercises God's authority in Christ Jesus.

Chapter Six

The War of Natures

Romans 5:12-8:39

What most people don't see in theological passages in the Bible, as we are looking at, is the supernatural behind the theology. As we examine the death in the old man through Adam and life in the new man through Christ Jesus; dead to sin and alive in Christ; the old man a slave, the new man free through righteousness; the war inside between the old and new man and our life, power, and glorification through the Holy Spirit, I will attempt to bring out the supernatural as we progress through the salvation to freedom texts. We will see how the power of God has and is dealing with our position in Christ and our condition in Adam.

Paul starts out by saying that when Adam sinned, he engaged in wrongdoing by willfully and morally transgressing God's law. He was acting contrary to God's will by choosing to go in an opposite direction to the way and course God had chosen for him. By choosing to obey Satan, Adam gave himself and humanity over to a governing principle where fundamentally we would live from a system of belief's and behavior that would start chains of reason, rooted and established in lies. Adam would find another nature working within his body that had power over him, and it brought forth sin. Sin would now have a seat, a permanent residence, in the will of man. Man would recognize sins seat because it would manifest itself in the conscience of humanity. Sin's power would be seen through human choices as he allowed his body to become an instrument for evil.

Adam would now determine what he considered lawful or not. Adam would no longer by nature have the ability to fulfill God's law. As long as we, the new creation, are trapped in our human body, the flesh, sins indwelling presence will continually produce lawlessness. Sin's nature comes from Satan and the fallen angels. If Satan, a metaphor for the fallen, have been sinning from the beginning, then it would be reasonable to say, the satanic principal is in dwelt within the old man, since we too sin. When Satan and the fallen rebelled, they contracted a judgment from God spoken over them throughout the ages upon ages. When Adam sinned, God spoke a curse over him, but also said He would redeem mankind through Christ Jesus.

When Adam sinned, sin entered the world or the entire human race and mankind began to sin. His sin spread death throughout all the created universe, so everything began to grow old and die. In Hebrews 1, the writer says God's throne is forever and He rules in righteousness. God created the heavens and the earth, but they will come to an end, they will all wear out like a garment, You (God) will roll them up like a robe and they will be changed like clothes. The creation waits in eager expectation when God does away with sin and the sons of God are fully revealed. When Paul says that death came from sin, he is talking about a process of dying. Sin brought immediate spiritual death, but physical death would be a process. Let me just add here, the laws of God we break through the sinful nature, bring spiritual consequences just as it did with Adam and Eve. These consequences could result in demonization, curses, sicknesses.

Paul reminds us that people sinned even before the law was given. People who lived between the time of Adam to Moses did not have any specific laws to break. Sin is first a person, then it is a power, thirdly, it is an act. Sin was in the world from the beginning, but it came into sharp focus when the law was given. Mankind began to perceive or become aware within the conscious and through his sense see a power that took advantage through the old man. It's desires to do evil wanted to grow and become further independent of God. Let me give us a realization that any student of the Bible faces in this book, the awareness that evil is indwell in the old man, visualized through physical death. The law of Moses still today, as it did in the Old

Testament, help people see their sinfulness. The law shows us the seriousness of our offenses, and to drive us to Christ for salvation and the forgiveness of sins. For Paul to write about this means that in his day it was still true. So the law points out our sin and places the responsibility for it on us. The law has no remedy, it just identifies the problem.

The contrast between Adam and Christ is the manifestation of the two selves, the old and new man. Adam's transgression determined the nature and character of time; Christ's one act of righteousness determined a nature and character for eternity. When Paul mentions the gift he is talking about justification through salvation in Christ Jesus. The opposite is found in the Adamic nature, condemnation. Death is the revelator of God's judgment on the sinful nature of man. Eternal life belongs to the new creation, the spirit and the soul. As we pursue righteousness, the new man, God's design for humanity, starts to produce good works that God has design from the beginning. Remember what Paul is describing concerning the old man. The old self is the product of deception, that is, of Satan's lie. That which denies the truth of God's Word. Deception then gave birth to lust, perverted damaging desires. When lust is yield too, it produces sin, and sin when it takes its course produces death. This is the scriptural degenerative process of the old man. The old man has two distinctive characteristics, first, it is corrupt (spiritually, morally, and physically), and secondly it is a rebel. This happen when God passed judgment on Adam's one sin of disobedience. This degenerative process has affected the entire human race and brought condemnation.

Paul takes this process one step further in Romans 5:17 stating that Adam caused death to rule over the whole human race. What the underlying point here is, death will rule over this evil age. But God's gift of righteousness through salvation in Christ Jesus takes us spiritually out of the realms of darkness and the control of the fallen angels and sets us free spiritually. We see the power of the new man in Christ as our minds are freed from the fallen angels through not being conformed to the pattern of this evil age or world. Conformed here means to be or become behaviorally or socially similar to the characteristics of the world. As our mind becomes set free from the fallen angels, the Holy Spirit begins to reestablish a mind responsive to Christ. The Holy Spirit desires to bring the mind of the one born again into glorification. To lift the mind into higher spheres, to enlarged the borders of meaning and truth. The renewed mind by the Holy Spirit starts to experience far deeper thought, mightier truths, and to express spiritual power.

When Adam sinned, mankind came under its power. The fallen angels having control within the old man's nature brought forth disobedience and condemnation. Sin has always brought forth heartache and punishment. Yet Christ's one act of righteousness, dying on the cross for the sins of the world, opened the way for all people to be made right in God's sight and to undergo sanctification. Sanctification is where the old nature lives no more, and the believer starts to live by the new creation, the new man. So the law was given to the Jew and for the whole human race, so that all people could see how sinful they are. Paul's argument in the first five chapters of Romans is that the law has made mankind aware of their need for salvation and to be delivered from the power of sin. We all know that this age is characterized by sin and a kingdom of evil who's power over the human race is sin; this inevitable brings death, but death can also be manifested in area's of human life. Christ bodily death and resurrection has positioned the believer to reign over sin and the evil powers of sin, bringing the believer into victory and eternal life. I have chosen these Biblical chapters so that the believer can see positional and conditional Christianity.

ROMANS 6

In reading Romans, chapters 1-5, Paul has shown people's need for salvation, the sin nature of humanity, sin and its power reigning over humanity. Paul reveals the need for salvation and the forgiveness of sins. In these next chapters we will see God's program for progressively separating believers from sin and its power and through the new man, making the believer more like Christ. Paul's key point will be that the believer has now another nature working within, the new man. The point will expand to the empowerment of the new man, found in the Holy Spirit. In chapters 6-7 Paul's focus will be the new nature against the old nature. Paul will show theologically how the kingdom of God through the Holy Spirit works within the believer and also how the kingdom of darkness works at the same time through the satanic principal, sin. Paul reveals that within the born again believer two kingdom coexist and are at war within; and so my title of this chapter.

Paul opens chapter six of Romans by saying, we should not take God's wonderful kindness in forgiving sin, to keep on willfully sinning. How God shows the believer more and more kindness is His grace through sanctification. Paul's point is, God's grace must not become and excuse to sin and to live immorally. We have died to sin positionally, and Paul says to tap the power of God's grace and be delivered from sin and the old man that sin operates through. Paul leaves open the idea that someone would claim to believe and yet plan on yielding to sin.

What is Paul's theological and spiritual concepts in chapters 6-7? In a legal sense and in a spiritual sense, the believer has died to sin. Through baptism, that is spiritually being buried with Christ we have died with Christ, and through Christ's resurrection we have been spiritually given a new life. Paul also says that in a moral since, sinful desires will be present, but they have been mortally wounded. The old man is powerless against the work of the Holy Spirit through the new man. Paul is saying the new man has the ability again to reflect the image and likeness of God. This only takes place as the believer learns to live from their position in Christ, disarming the fallen angels, principalities and powers in the heavenly realm.

Baptism is a metaphor or an analogy of a spiritual truth. We know from scriptural foundations that baptism is an act of a believer who has decided to follow Christ. Paul pictures how Jesus died for sin, we positionally also died to a sinful lifestyle, so that the power of the Holy Spirit can produce in us the new creation and lifestyle. Going under the water is a powerful picture. It is spiritually a picture of Jesus breaking the powers of the fallen angels and demons over the believers life positionally. This is why many times when a person is baptized by power ministries, deliverance and healing's takes place. The baptized person comes up out of the water speaking in a heavenly language. So positionally the believer has the power to be free, but conditionally through the flesh, there is a nature and power that must be executed. Theologically, baptism represents the death of the old man and that way of life. It represents being raised in Christ to a new life like His.

Christ's agony of death and His glorious resurrection united us in Him and then coming to the understanding that dying to sin is going to be painful and a lifelong process. Being raised with Christ is more that theological, it is the power of God creating. Authority will always be seen in power. The believer who exercises their position over their condition, is the believer who is putting to death the old man, and living in power through the new man.

We must divide the Word of God scripturally as long as it is balanced with power. Jesus' death rendered sin powerless. Power is a person, just as sin is a nature. We must never lose spiritual realities as we venture through theological passages in the Bible. Where theology is, so is authority and power. It may not be visible like healing and deliverance, but it is behind the seen upholding theology. For example, when Paul says that through the new man we are no longer slaves to sin, he is speaking positionally. He is saying, we are to exercise our transformed mind over sin or we are to be delivered from persons of sin, in either case, theology and spiritual ministry are working hand in hand. Remember we do not war against flesh and blood, but against spiritual forces of evil without bodies.

Freedom was rare in Biblical times except through death. Death brings about a release that cannot be reversed. Paul's spiritual reality is that as we die to sin and its power (person), we are free to live for Christ. Evil spirit's desire control through sins power, just as freedom in Christ the Holy Spirit desires control to bring about God's image and likeness. Evil thoughts and action reveal who the evil spirit is and what he likes. When Jesus died and defeated the kingdom of darkness, evil spirits through sin are render powerless as the believer exercises their new man over the old man in all scriptural processes.

When Paul says we have been identified with Christ, he is referring to who and what someone is. This starts in the mind, where the seat of sin is, where the fallen angels have control. As our minds become renewed in Christ, we recognize and distinguish the difference between the new man and the old man. As we come into association with Christ our identity changes in thought and action. We start to share the same characteristics as Christ. In our mind we desire the things of God because we are no longer yielding our minds to earthly sinful behavior. Paul asks a major question here, if we are dead to sin, how can sin still control us? Theologically, we have died to sin according to the new man, but according to the old man we are constantly being freed from the desire to sin. Spiritual we are being delivered by our choices or being exorcised from evil.

Authors owe the body of Christ the whole truth, not just writing from a theological or spiritual perspective, but both. The truth is, if people have such a desire and given in to its lustful desires, then deliverance is the only scriptural method for freedom. If we can say no to sin and it's over, then the power of free will has repelled evil. Because sin has a power within the believers soul, we will have the compulsion to sin in the body. I like Paul, desire to be freed from the sinful nature, yet God has chosen the process of sanctification, so I must too. I do understand that our wrestling match with sin is design to bring about the power of free will in the new creation, in God's wisdom, this too is part of our glorification. We must understand that as we live in these mortal bodies, the lower nature, we do have the power to no longer let sin control us. Again, if we cannot say no to sin, then a evil spirit through sin must be exorcised.

Paul says, because our mortal decaying bodies are dying, revealing that the old man lives under curses, we should not yield to those sinful desires and temptation coming from demons and fallen angels. Our freedom is found as we give ourselves completely to God and use our whole bodies as tools to do what is right. If we have a choice, then we have been given the power of the new life, and the kingdom of darkness can only do what we permit or obey. Paul says the God's desire in Christ Jesus is that sin will not ever again be our master. Master implies a person, and sin manifests a power. We are not subject to the law or bound as prisoners to the law in the new man. Yet the new man is being freed from the law. The law is revealing sin and evil that operates through sin. True reality, the law produces both the proof and the acute awareness of evil spirits through sin, directing and guiding the individual's into sins captivity. Paul ends this half of the chapter saying that God's grace, God's forgiveness of sin and His willingness to deliver us from evil will overcome as the believer pursues scriptural procedure.

FREEDOM TO OBEY GOD'S SPIRIT

Paul begins this part of scripture in almost the same way as the last one. He wants us to have no misunderstanding, in a believers life there are two masters, sin and the evil spirit behind the sin and the Lord Jesus Christ with the power of the Holy Spirit. The law of God has never been against God's grace, but it came along side to reveal sin, and the power of the person or evil spirit working behind sins desires and actions.

Verse one and fifteen seem to almost repeat the question and Paul response is of the same manner. Paul says, willfully sinning will never bring about God's grace or opportunity to exercise more grace. What willfully sinning does is reveal the power of sin in the old man and very likely uncover evil spirit behind that sin. This is seen in verse sixteen of chapter six. As Christians, the righteousness or the sinfulness that we obey shows how much we are surrendered to light, darkness, or a little of both. Paul says we are a slave to whomever or whatever we commit ourselves to obey, in the visible or invisible realms.

When sin becomes someones master, that individual has no power except to obey what it bids through desire and action. But when we choose to obey God, we become slaves of obedience. There is only two choices, obey God and walk out our salvation or obey the devil and live under his bondage. We all were at one time slaves to sin and the devil, since he has been sinning from the beginning. The old man has the nature and desires of the devil, and through deception and lies, leads us into bondage. The new man was a creative act of God that response to truth, righteousness, and holiness. Let me say it this way, service to sin and the devil leaves us into captivity and death, service to God and truth, leads us into righteousness and eternal life.

The power of the new man is from the Holy Spirit, but there is also an equal power, the Word of God. Paul says that the Word of God acts like a master keeping us free from sin and the power of the kingdom of darkness. We are no longer living as slaves to sin, but living as slaves to righteousness, experiencing the Kingdom of God. In verse nineteen, the old man is weak, vulnerable to the kingdom of darkness that brings spiritual dishonor and possession. When believers are slaves to impurity and lawlessness, two spiritual categories, they are held in bondage through the old man by spiritual forces of wickedness in the heavenly realms and in the terrestrial realms.

It is God's will through the new man to have benefits of the Kingdom immeasurably. These spiritual blessing come in two levels! The believer who in born again, filled with the Holy Spirit and speaking in tongues, and is a student and doer of the Word will experience blessing in accordance to living from the new man and how much the old man is not active. The second level is far more of an outpouring of blessing in extreme measure as the believer does the first step, but adds deliverance from the legal rights and curses accrued in their life and past generations. There is a powerful difference between the two, but as evil spirits lose their right to block blessings, this believer receives showers of blessing.

When Paul mentions the law, he is referring to a system of laws, civil statutes, and priestly ordinances within the Mosaic covenant as a means of God's favor or blessing. Simply put, we do not purposely go out and break the law, for God's Word will stand forever. The believer cannot become righteous through the law, but can willfully or through choice be condemn in the old man though the law. How is that possible? The law itself is not evil, but it does tell us what evil is. There is something else the law will do, it will arouse evil desires. Paul says without the law he would not have known what lust or coveting was. We really must be careful when the law says thou shall not. It is through the old man as I have said before that the kingdom of darkness seeks access for possession. So when the Bible says, thou shall not or do not mark your skin with tattoos, through the old man, evil enters for possession. The body becomes demonized and the soul oppressed. Paul said that no sooner had he become aware of that commandment then it awaken from a sleep if we will, feelings, emotions, and responses forbidden from within him. This nonsense that evil spirits attach themselves to believers because a Christian cannot have a demon, that one needs to go back to the Bible and the school of the supernatural and gather correct theology. What Paul is saying so argumentatively is that when the law said thou shall not lust, the law introduce him to some of the darkest emotions and desires. Supernaturally, it introduced him too many realms of evil spirits.

The new man realizes the seriousness of the law and the evil spirits of sin and their power through the old man. In second heaven deliverance, I find this truth to be true, and through the old man breaking the laws of God, fallen angels accuse us in the courts of heaven. It is through the old man that they have their rights and curses from the creation. If I live a life of pornography and a life for Christ, the old man is alive and evil spirits have me captive. If through the new man I ask Jesus to deliver me from evil, those spirits are exorcised and that part of the old man dies. The new man thrives at the expense of the old man. Sin finds its power through the commandment, there is nothing wrong with the commandment, but sin live through the old man.

Paul treats the law like a legal binding contract from God. He says the law is holy, righteous or right, and good. Believers must understand Paul and the other Apostles concerning the law, it reflects God's nature, character and His will. The commandment defines sin and also reveals how evil spirits are defeated. Many times I will take someone who has a lot of sexual immorality in their past and in their generations through curse breaking accord to the law of Mose. One thing I have found in dealing with evil spirits, whether Old or New Testament, "it is written" does them in.

The new man loves the laws of God, not for righteousness, but for power and authority in Christ Jesus. The new man desires to follow God's Word, for in it, the new man sees what God's purpose is for him. That purpose bring within destiny, God's image and likeness to rule again in authority. Satan and sin may have frustrated man, but now the new creation in Christ has destiny and purpose with authority and power. This is why Paul cries out, who will rescue me from this body of sin and death.

STRUGGLE WITH SIN & EVIL

We see from the early Church that they held the law of God in high regard. We as the body of Christ mostly have a different view. We say things like, I'm not under the law, as a way or attitude of disrespect or something as treating the law casually. Paul made an effort to clarify between God's holy law, sin, and the new creation. This view in the proper perspective or viewpoint. If our outlook is not based on those three points, we can quickly fall into doctrinal or supernatural error. We can quickly think that the cross took care of everything and it doesn't really matter what I do, Jesus will forgive. This statement is a half truth and a half lie. How can we be free from sin in Christ Jesus and continue to openly sin? In Christ, we are spiritually free from sin, that is our position. In the flesh, sin has an indwell throne in the seat of the human soul. The believer in Christ spiritually is free from the penalty of sin and judgment. The believer is also free spiritually free from sin power of the evil spirits. But while still in the flesh, are sinful nature reveals in the body we are not free from the temptation of evil spirits and sin. The wake up care to the believer is that Paul never claimed that being under grace and not under law meant that we somehow were above the law. Hard and cold statement, conditionally were are judged by the law, that is conditionally. Spiritually, we are set free from the law and the power of the transformed mind brings this reality into a fallen and evil age. Let me say it this way, the trouble is not God's law, but me.

Paul now reveals his own personal dilemma and invites us to look deeper into our own behavior and understanding of the two selves. Paul shows that while we are in this evil age, the fallen angels have power over that lower nature of sin, just as the Holy Spirit has control and power over the born again human spirit.

Paul gives us three powerful lessons he realized in dealing with the old man. One, scriptural knowledge of the law is not the answer. Two, any type of self determination or to want to do right will not bring lasting change. Three, being a Christian does not conditionally wipe out sin and possession of evil spirit. The baptism of the Holy Spirit is not about speaking in tongues, the for the empower to bring sanctification conditionally or in the flesh. The Holy Spirit is the one who sets us free from sin and evil spirits who enter through sin. Paul gets unbelievable real in Romans 7:16-17. He says it is sin, that is the nature of

Satan, inside me that makes me do these evil things the law forbids. Paul says there is a conflict inside him, he wants to do what the law requires, but there is this lower sinful nature that prevents him. He is advocating support for understanding the law and not purposely breaking the law and so many believers do.

We realize that our sinful nature is a part of our being and there is nothing holy, righteous, or good in it. Although we belong to Christ and have died to sin positionally, we still conditionally live is a sinful body and a sinful world. Paul describes the person who tries to do good and has the desire to do good, but can't. Paul says, without the Holy Spirit's aid, there will be no process of death to the old man. Paul says believers love God's law and His ways. They should desire and put into action the things God has for them. But this other law at work within the lower nature keeps the believer from many of the blessings of God.

The believer must know that these two powers within, the Holy Spirit and the satanic principal are not equal, but they are both there. The satanic principal dwelling within the human soul and body, must be executed. If the believer cannot say no to sin, then the believer must come to the truth, through the satanic principal evil spirits have accessed your body and are working against the Holy Spirits sanctification process through our yielding by choices. As long as we are here on earth, our mortal bodies are bodies of death. The soul of the believer is being renewed or if need be, being expelled of fallen angels who have access be nature.

The struggle is real! The victories in Christ Jesus by the Holy Spirit are sweet and joyful. Many believers don't see themselves truthfully, and so don't appreciate what they have in Christ so they never scripturally obtain every spiritual blessings in the heavenly realms.

THE VICTORIES LIFE IN THE SPIRIT

The believer who can fully understand Paul, both positionally and conditionally, understands that the believers blessings and power are in the new man. In the new man there is no condemnation in Christ, because Christ was punished by death on a cross for us. Yet, through the old man, condemnation is all he produces. The victory of the new man is found when the believer starts to deal with the past sin, curses, and even generational issues. Every Holy Spirit believer understands that the power of the fallen is in the choices of all generations. As the power of demonic spirits are in the words and deeds of all generations. These are facts I've learned in 22 years of demonic deliverance and 10 years of fallen angel judgments. Again, we are not condemned spiritually, but in the flesh, there are spiritual iniquities that condemn us. What is Paul's answer for us? The power of the life giving Holy Spirit has set us free from the law of sin and death. If we look closely, this is two-fold! Spiritually, we have become alive in Christ and set free from eternal death immediately. But to be set free from the law is different. Positionally we are set free from the law and conditionally we are being set free from the law. Freedom from the law is a sanctification process, but the power of sanctification is found in identification. Identification is the legal side of our redemption. It unveils to us what God did in Christ for us, from the time Jesus went to the cross, until He sat down on the right hand of the Father. Paul says in Galatians, "I have been crucified WITH CHRIST." We died WITH Christ and that we were buried WITH Christ. This is one of the great keys that unlocks the teaching of the old man and new man. Paul says that Christ became one with us in sin, that we might become one WITH Jesus in righteousness. In Ephesians 2:6, "And raised us up WITH him, and made us to sit WITH him in the heavenly places, in Christ Jesus. This and other scriptures reveal our legal side, and it is in our legal side that we defeat the fallen angels. It is in our sanctification side that we are set free from demonic spirits. Colossians 2:13, "And you, being dead through your trespasses and the uncircumcision of your flesh, you I say, did he make alive together WITH Him." Romans 6:5, "for if we have become united WITH him in the likeness of his death, we shall be also in the likeness of his resurrection."

In Romans 8:3,4 says, God sent His own Son in a human body like ours, except that ours are sinful, and destroyed sin's control and power over us by giving Himself as a sacrifice for our sins. It is through this sanctification process that we now can obey God's law if we follow after the Holy Spirit and no longer obey the old evil nature within us.

Those who choose to let themselves be controlled by their old man, that lower nature, live only to please that satanic principal. But following after the Holy Spirit, we find ourselves doing those things that please God, and it brings us life and peace. Yet, the old man within us is against God and it will never obey God's laws and those things that bring blessing. That is why those who are still under the control of their old man, Satan's will, are bent on following their old man with its evil desires, can never please God.

I am writing in this manner to bring to light what is hidden in darkness. We understand this in some form theologically, but most are clueless spiritually. The key to understanding the New Testament is understanding theologically and supernaturally the old man and new man.

We if filled with the Holy Spirit are not like that. We don't follow after the old man, because we are controlled by the new man, which is the power of the life in Christ through the Holy Spirit. Even though Christ dwells in our spirit man, the new man, our bodies that house the old man will die because of sin, the satanic principal. Here is a powerful principal that needs some thought; if the Spirit of God who raised up Jesus dwell in the new man, the Holy Spirit will make our dying bodies live again after we die. Spiritually, if the Holy Spirit has been granted through the work of Christ to resurrect our human bodies, then He today has a legal right to heal and deliver these dying bodies.

The new man has no obligations whatsoever to the old man to do what the old man desires. The sinful desires acted on bring demonization and sickness. Paul says it we keep on following the old man, we perish, now and possibly for eternity. But through the new man and the power of the Holy Spirit we crush the old man and the satanic principal (nature of the devil) we will live and be blessed. Why? Because through the new man empower by the Holy Spirit we are led and we enter into sonship in Christ. This is why we are to grow up into our salvation or grow up into the new man, who is the image of Christ's likeness.

The new man behaves like God's children, one who is experiencing their adoption and the family, calling God Father! God's Holy Spirit speaks to us deep within our new man, the heart, and tell us what we really are, empowered again to live for God through the Christ's life. This means restoring God's image and likeness in the creation. Since we are child through the new man, we now and will share in God's treasures, because all God gave to His Son Jesus, in Christ we were and are to experience that treasure. The truth treasure through the new man is the fullness of Christ Jesus. This is the reason God saved mankind, that through Jesus mankind would restore God's image, likeness, and authority in the earth. This is what it means to share in His glory, coming into the fullness of the new man, which is the image and likeness of Christ Jesus.

Even if we have to suffer in this tent, the old man, putting of the old creation, both spiritually and conditionally. Living from the new man and coming into the fullness of the new man cannot compare to the glory God is giving and will give in the new man. We should realized all creation is waiting patiently and hopefully for that future day. But the creation is responding today to the glory of the new man as he progress and is molded into the image of Christ. As Christ is formed in us, sickness has less and less effect, just as sin does. This is a true reality! As the body of Christ becomes a bunch of children (new man), those children become one new man corporately. The creation, notice the word creation, visible and invisible Paul refers too, waits with expectation for the sons of God to be revealed. I do understand the future intent here, but the kingdom and sonship is now, so the creation undergoes measures of transformation as the sons exercise God's authority and power through His likeness and image. This is how the fallen angels are taken out. As principalities (regions of land) principalities in the second heaven are dethroned. As Jesus commanded the creation, the creation is ready to respond to the believer or believers who are transformed into the Christ likeness, the new man!

The whole creation is suffering or groaning in sins agony! We Christians have the Holy Spirit within us as we foretaste the futures glory by releasing that glory today! Because we are tasting the power and authority in our new man, we burn with passion and anxiously wait for that day when God will give us our full rights as His children, including the new bodies governed by the new nature as He promised us. These new bodies that we will have in the future is promised never to be sick again or die because of sin. We all know this to be true, so the Holy Spirit through the new man is working on us so that we can have many measure of that fulfillment. We are experiencing our salvation in measures today!

In our new man by faith, the Holy Spirit helps us with our daily problems and weakness knowing that all things are working out for the good as we pursue growth in the new man. This is God's purpose, the believer and the corporate believers coming into the power of sonship, which is the new man.

I will close this book with one last point that is of great importance! As we might notice, I closed the last chapter with this same thought. The purpose of God in bringing forth many children is to bring a collective body of believers as one new man as stated in Ephesians 2:14-15.

> *For He Himself is our peace, who made both groups into one and broke down the barrier of the dividing wall, by abolishing in His flesh the enmity, which is the Law of commandments contained in ordinances, so that in Himself He might make the two into one new man, thus establishing peace. Ephesians 2:14-15 NASB*

God's overall purpose for the new man is a body of believers operating as one new man. This cannot happen unless the Church turns back to the Holy Spirit. God's design is for the new man to operate through a corporative body, the Church, to bring forth His likeness and authority. Notice Ephesians 4:16, from whom the whole body, being fitted and held together by what every joint supplies, according to the proper working of each individual part, causes the growth of the body for the building up of itself in love.

We are to be one complete corporate body, expressing one new corporate man. This new man is to reenact Christ earthly ministry and in so doing fulfills God's two purposes, revealing God to the world and exercises God's authority in Christ Jesus. By God's design, from the new man God's authority and power will bring a harvest of daunting proportions through the preaching of the gospel with sign and wonders. As the collective new man goes forward, the original purpose from the garden of eden is reinstated. Be fruitful in Christ and multiply as disciples and fill the earth by subduing it in God's likeness and authority!

"Behold, I (Jesus) am coming quickly, and My reward is with Me, to give to each one according to the merit of his deeds (earthly works, faithfulness). I am the Alpha and the Omega, the First and the Last, the Beginning and the End [the Eternal One]." Revelation 22:12-13

Blessed (happy, prosperous, to be admired) are those who wash their robes [in the blood of Christ by believing and trusting in Him—the righteous who do His commandments], so that they may have the right to the tree of life, and may enter by the gates into the city. Revelation 22:14

CHAPTER SEVEN

POWER OF THE NEW MAN OVER FALLEN ANGELS

I don't think the believer really knows how much power God has placed inside the new man. Within the new man, there are no limitations to the believer as he follows the Holy Spirit. The Holy Spirit spoke years ago and said, "you're only limitation is Me."

He was telling me that if I do as He says, the impossible that was in the old man, now becomes the possible in the new man. Jesus was manifested to model what God has planned for the new man. Through the new creation the believer would be invited into the spirit realm where miracles, healings, and deliverance would be the norm! God can do anything or use anyone to do anything, but consistency into a lifestyle is the development of the new man.

"How God anointed Jesus of Nazareth with the Holy Spirit and with great power; and He went around doing good and healing all who were oppressed by the devil, because God was with Him." Acts 10:38

In 2 Peter 2:10-11, scripture says, celestial beings (second heaven fallen angels) and God's angels are stronger and more powerful than mankind. In my first book we talk about the falsity of angels turning into demons when they sinned and fell. We as human beings stayed human when we fell. In both cases, it is the nature that fell. Recapturing the truth about the restoration of the new man will bring the harvest of souls during the end times.

God anointed Jesus with a task that was to bring supernatural blessings to mankind. Jesus was anointed, which means to operate in God's authority and power. The anointing has two main functions. One, the ability to bring about blessings as appointed by God in many different area's. Two, to bring about supernatural sanctions upon the kingdom of darkness. This means that the anointing imposes penalties for conduct and actions which restricts the overall operations of the kingdom of darkness.

God is changing the way believers think about the end time harvest. God is moving the Church toward the deliverance ministry so that the reality of the Kingdom of God defeats darkness. So far the Church has done very little to restrict evil. The Churches focus has been on God's power in the earth, but it does not recognize the reality of fallen angels, who have legal rights in the earth. Right now we have a lot of revivalist who are moving in healing, but know little concerning the authority and power of the second heaven. The more the Church embraces correct fallen angel deliverance, quicker the harvest will come. The results will be impressive outpourings of the Holy Spirit with miracles, healings, deliverances of demons and the defeat of evil in territories. If the believer is to live a normal Christian life, spiritual warfare will have to be embrace as much or more than the healing movement.

A New Reality

In the book of Revelation, when Jesus is addressing the Churches, He uses the word 'overcomes.' Jesus is speaking to church members in any age and directing them to fulfill the purposes of God in the world. So, the Greek word for overcome is 'nikao,' which means "to conquer." It is a warfare term commonly used by the Greek's. The Dictionary of New Testament Theology says, "New Testament usage of the word group almost always presupposes the conflict between God or Christ and opposing demonic powers." In Revelation 2 & 3, seven times Jesus tells His people to overcome by engaging in spiritual warfare. If the believer does this that one should expect to receive substantial rewards from Christ.

Today when someone mentions spiritual warfare, most believers think about casting out demons. There is another definition of 'nikao' from 'Strongs' that must be mentioned. It is when one is arraigned or goes to a court of law, to win the case or to maintain one's cause. This definition has to do with the fallen angels. Every fallen angel has been in God's courtroom to accuse our family bloodline, people group, Church, organization, city, state, nation, the world. The word arraigned means to bring someone before a court to answer for criminal charges with the purpose of finding fault to condemn. This is exactly what the fallen angels do concerning humanity. The fallen angels through the sinful nature of humanity, accuses both believers and non-believers of crimes committed against God's law. When these fallen angels come down by God's command, it is God's intent to have them judged according to the works of Christ Jesus who fulfilled the law and the believers position in Christ. As stated before, the old man has its origin in the satanic nature. The new man in Christ Jesus. We must remember, Paul says the law has two functions. First, it was given to show people how guilty they are; meaning that God had given the law to punish sin. Second, the law reveals the nature and will of God and shows people how to live; the law is an aid to guard and protect people from the fallen angels. The law cannot make people righteous, but it is a tool in the hands of the Holy Spirit to show humanity sin. Paul plainly explains that the promises of God came to Abraham, but the law was given to angels to give to Moses, who was the mediator between God and the people.

On mount Sinai God called the whole creation into account by giving the law through the angels of God to mankind. God also called the evil fallen angels and had them witness the contract made with humanity. This is not a new idea, but a long history of Jewish belief. Even Acts

7:53 confirms, Jews believed the Ten Commandments had been given to Moses by God through or witnessed by angels. I can take this one step further in Jesus' power encounter with the devil and the fallen angels in the wilderness. In the temptation of Jesus, He always answered the devil, and the fallen with, "it is written." In over one thousand fallen angel power encounters, the Holy Spirit gives scripture to answer the fallen angels accusations. Once the fallen's accusations have been answered according to our scriptural position in Christ, he and his kind pull out of the mind, then the demons come out of the body automatically.

Ephesians 1:19-23, Paul prayed that the Church would understand the incredible greatness of God's power for us who believe in Him. The power of the new man (new creation) is found when God raised Christ Jesus from the dead and seated Him at God's right hand. Notice where Jesus is seated, at God's right hand in the heavenly realms. There is something else that is extremely powerful. Christ Jesus is far above all rule and authority, power and dominion, and notice, every title that can be given. Paul is speaking about the authority over humanity, the creation, and the fallen angels. This authority to rule is not only in this present evil age but also in the age to come. God placed all things under Christ Jesus' authority and appointed Him to be Head over everything for the Church, which is His body. The Church has been called to come into the fullness of Christ who He Himself fills everything in every way. Yes, the Church is to exercise such power over the fallen angels that humanity returns to Jesus. When Paul states we have been raised up with Christ in Ephesians 2:6, the Church now has power through proper spiritual warfare tactics against the fallen angels that humanity gets saved, sins power undergoes a breaking, and the creation responds to righteousness.

Territorial fallen angels are not afraid of ministries who do not understand this revelation by using Christ's reign. Most Church leaders are okay with the outpouring of the Holy Spirit, and believe God's move is here. This half truth leads the believer into Holy Spirit encounters through their spirit man, the new creation, but leaves the old man, the satanic principal, possessed with demons and under the control of territorial spirits. Anyone with spiritual warfare understanding knows the two realms of humanity and ministers to both the old man and the new man.

> I have told you these things, so that in Me you may have [perfect] peace. In the world you have tribulation and distress and suffering, but be courageous [be confident, be undaunted, be filled with joy]; I have overcome the world." [My conquest is accomplished, My victory abiding.] John 16:33 Amplified

If Christ is in us, and we are in Him, then as Jesus defeated the prince fallen angel Satan, then Jesus is the perfect prototype of the one who overcomes. Jesus is saying, through perfect obedience and the word of God, I defeated the devil and the fallen in God's courts every time. Jesus did this even by laying down His life willfully, to die for the sins of the world as the lamb sacrificed. The willful choice of the cross broke the fallen angel's power over the mind of humanity. In my first book, demons are personal issues, and fallen angels are humanity's problems. Spiritual warfare has no questions of who will overcome, the question is, proper spiritual warfare tactics.

> *But even if our gospel is [in some sense] hidden [behind a veil], it is hidden [only] to those who are perishing; among them the god of this world [Satan] has blinded the minds of the unbelieving to prevent them from seeing the illuminating light of the gospel of the glory of Christ, who is the image of God. 2 Corinthians 4:3-4 Amplified*

Paul says through spiritual warfare encounters with the second heaven fallen angels, their job is to put a veil over the minds of mankind. I understand Paul is talking about the lost, but there is more here than meets the eye. The one who is trained in second heaven fallen angel deliverance knows fallen angels blind the minds of all humanity. It is my personal experience ministering too many in second heaven deliverance is the only way that veil or blindness is removed. This may shock some, but the reality of the unbelieving mind is the fallen angel's power. Just look at all the unbelief in the Church. Maybe there is unbelief in what I said. The design of the new man is to be illuminated, to see through the gospel the glory of all that Jesus accomplished. The new man sees God's image in Christ and our ability through the new man to carry that image in jars of clay. This brings the downfall of the fallen angels as Jesus did, and His life displayed.

When someone goes through second heaven deliverance, pressure from the neck up, headaches, confusion, difficulty concentrating, nausea or motion sickness and dizziness happen until free; a veil pulled off their head; a mask taken off; like a vacuum hooked up to the head; the daunting lies leave; a band around the head breaks when the fallen loose the mind. These are just some manifestations of the second heaven fallen angel deliverance. What is the result besides the quiet mind, the person can see the gospel with a new understanding?

As I have said before, the war will continue until the end of this evil age. To live as Jesus command us to live as a believer, we become active and aggressive Christians, and we find ourselves in constant warfare.

Jesus also used the Greek word 'nikao' in the New Testament in the book of Luke, 11:21-22. Jesus speaks of overcoming the strongman. First, we must ask ourselves who is the strongman? The strongman Jesus is talking about is the fallen angel Satan. Satan's house is his kingdom or where sin reigns. Most spiritual warfare writers say these scriptures speak about casting out of demons. On the surface they are right! Jesus is talking about the terrestrial realm and the celestial realm at the same time. In the terrestrial or earthly realm, there is a strongman or chief spirit of the body. But, the deeper meaning is that the chief demonic strongman works for the fallen angel above him, and he the fallen angel works for the hierarchy, up to include Satan. The Pharisees contributed this miracle through demonic deliverance to Beelzebub or Satan. I also know

Beelzebub could talk about a fallen angel who is ruler of demons under his command. So, Satan has a kingdom as a strongman; fallen angels have demons who do their work are also strongmen; and there are chief demons who are strongmen. Within the hierarchy of evil, terrestrial or celestial, there are many strongmen.

Anyone who has had a spiritual warfare encounter with Beelzebub understands that that name comes on all three levels. It could be a chief demon, a fallen angel, or Satan himself. But to write that Beelzebub is one of the highest ranking principalities in the invisible world of darkness is just not so. When people write about things like this in spiritual warfare strategy, it quickly tells me they have never faced Beelzebub on all combat levels. In that book, the author even says Beelzebub is not Satan. The problem with statements like this, it is presumptuous. Any spiritual warrior who has faced Satan in combat knows, he comes in all the names the Bible gives him. Remember, those that write about demonic principalities are in error as far as their terminology. If their terminology is wrong, then you can be sure that they have never been in live combat with a fallen angel. From the jump, from the first time I first encountered a fallen angel in live combat, he addressed himself as fallen, not a demon. Over one thousand times this has been the case. I ask when not sure, are you a demon or are you fallen? Lie not to the Holy Spirit! Those who speak about demonic principalities have had their hypotheses strongly influenced by their paradigm. This has also happened when writers talk about going into the courts of heaven concerning demons. I do understand about prayer in the courts of heaven, but spiritual warfare in the Bible has to do with combat.

I do want to say one more thing before we move on. It is possible to receive selected, but well founded, information from evil spirits under attack. This is where God's angels come to the aid and force evil spirit to tell what needs to be said. We also know that we must exercise careful discernment while attempting to extract information knowing that evil spirits deceive.

THE NEW MAN DEFEATING FALLEN ANGELS

When we talk about upper level spiritual warfare, many authors and deliverance ministers label it cosmic level warfare or strategic level warfare. Even though I fully understand what they are talking about, their description does not accurately describe second heaven warfare. The name the dark evil angels use is "fallen." These writers and deliverance ministers also say there are at least five kinds of higher level satanic spirits, or fallen angels. I find their categories or classifications incorrect or incomplete! They list territorial spirits which is a correct classification, but there are many levels of territorial spirits. The territorial fallen angels are thrones, dominions, principalities and powers. Within each of these four levels, there are at least nine different fallen angels who are tiered and sub-rule according to their creative order or number. Institutional fallen angels are over the Masonic Lodge as an example, organization if you will, and even over powerless Churches is also a correct category. The next listed is vice spirits, this is incorrect. Demons are vice spirits, fallen angels are all about the mind. Some talk about household spirits, this too is demonic spirits and not fallen angels. Fallen angels are all about the bloodline, the course of an age, and the mind. The last one is ancestor spirits, this depends on how one would describe it. If a demon, then incorrect, if fallen and the control of the mind, then correct. We must remember that fallen angels are all about the direction and course of this evil age. They are over family bloodlines, institutions, Churches, territory, even over the world. I have pictures in chapter ten to help the reader.

We are not to be confused by whom is at work. Satan and the fallen angels are at work in the four different dimensions of the second heaven where demons are at work in the earth. There are different levels of demons, and that is determined by who the sire or father was. There are also many different levels of fallen angels, and that is determined by their creative order. I will continue to remind you due to the newness of the material. These books are not revelations, but spiritual warfare combat encounters proven with over one thousand encounters.

The goal of the new creation, the individual and the corporate body, is to engage in demonic deliverance or ground level warfare until it forces the fallen angels or the cosmic levels to come down and defend their soldiers, the demons. Remember earlier I said fallen angels are faithful to to defend different levels of demonic spirits. The fallen angels know certain witchcraft spirits, blood right demons, and sexual vice demons they need to protect. They will come down and protect their army of demons. This insures the family line stays demonized. The army of evil, fallen or demonic, is their partnership with humanity. It is the Churches function to engage demons in such a way that the fallen angels assignment is threatened and forces them to come down and face the individual or Church.

When people have been entangled with Freemasonry, Scientology, Mormonism, Jehovah Witness, Islam, New Age, or any other religion, demon possession is automatic. Yet the fallen angels over those false religions control the demonization of the people and the territorial rights to the land. When people commit abortion, demonization is automatic, but again it is the ruling fallen angel who assigns the possession and to the degree. This is also true with the LGBT community! We must not forget, demonic spirits and fallen angel infirmities are also assigned. Here is a clue to the complexity of the structure of darkness, some demonic spirits don't have to come forward or manifest unless specially asked for. This too is a design to keep the bloodline under guard.

Today's spiritual warfare writers say they do not know or are unclear as to the war going on with fallen angels. This should not be so. The Church must put such pressure on the demonic realm to force a war with the fallen angels over that bloodline, Church, institution, county, state, country, continent, world, universe. They say we can assume that there is war in the heavenlies, but could it be that these writers are under the control of the fallen angels because they have not pursued the war in the way it is to be fought? The Bible is clear, that fallen angels must be judged in God's courtroom, Psalm 82. If it is a fallen angel over a sickness or bloodline, then the Apostle Peter clarifies that that fallen angel must be judged and sent to tartaros!

In dealing with fallen angels over a city, they release only those who meet the conditions. The same is true with institutions such as Freemasonry! Let me give an example, God judged in a ministry session a fallen angel over the cities region who was Freemasonry, and everyone who had Masonic Lodge in the family line fell out in the meeting as that fallen angel pulled out of the minds of those present and then the believers automatically coughed up demons. Point, when the fallen come under judgment, demons under their command come out as well. The second Peter account is so miss read in the Church. The pits of gloom or darkness assigned is that realm of darkness for judgment. I must enforce that scripture just like every other scripture. The lack of understanding that has happened in the Church because of need of spiritual warfare encounters is extreme. That word hell in the Amplified Bible is the Greek word tartaros. This realm is not the same place as hell or sheol. It is assigned specifically for the fallen angels. To the one who reads 2 Peter 2:4, 'For if God did not [even] spare angels that sinned, but threw them into hell and sent them to pits of gloom to be kept [there] for judgment;' quickly assumes that God has already placed fallen angels there. But the key word here is for judgment. I am to engage in second heaven combat when God send them down or they come on their own, have them judged according to the believers position in Christ. Once the courtroom of God has ruled, then the believer or Church is to have that fallen angel bound with eternal chains of darkness for the judgment, and then pray Psalm 82. God then and forever sends them to tartaros. We will talk more about this later in the book, but this is the overall process I have been doing individually and corporately over ten years. If this is new to you, I have said before, this is the next generation deliverance.

The vastness of this war is almost endless if we depend on individual deliverance ministries to handle this. This war according to apostolic writings is the Churches responsibility. These fallen angelic majesties all over the world have many rulers and sub-rules in the different sphere of authority according to their rank or created number. Bible dictionaries define these evil angelic majesties as first ones, preeminent ones, leaders. This means they are from the beginning, chief in order, time and place or rank. They call themselves the ancient ones; their rank is chief prince, prince, king, and captain. Within that structure there are sub-rulers, or sub-rulers within those titles. Most of these high level evil angelic majesties call themselves some title of Jesus. The fallen angels do not have demonic names and look at demons as inferior in creation.

When the fallen angels come down, there is pressure from the neck up, headaches, dizziness, confusion, difficulty concentrating, experience nausea similar to motion sickness as stated earlier. Notice the fallen affect the mind. The mind comes under the influence and the fight can be very difficult for the believer even to talk or remember what they say. This is when I ask God for His angels to come down and disarm the strongman (fallen angel). This seems to weaken them. I say something like, Father in Jesus' name, it is written to disarm the strongman, so I ask that you order the strongman to be disarmed of the Satanic armor. Then I pray that the fallen angel is made to say what is the certificate of debts the family bloodline owes the fallen angel or what is the debts the fallen angel has. I make a list, and then I pray to counter those debts with the works of Jesus for mankind. In prayer I am seeking all the fallen angels goods or possession as written in Luke 11. The deliverance scriptures in the Bible are powerful against the fallen. Again, once the process is complete, I read Psalm 82, the fallen angel pulls out of the mind, and the person coughs up demons. If this does not happen, the fallen and the demons have not left. Over one thousand encounters have proven this to be true!

Dream, revelation, the prophetic, words of knowledge, and prayer in the courts of heaven for deliverance is only in part, that is Bible. Non confrontational is only getting what has been legally covered, but confrontational deliverance makes evil spirits forcefully give over what they don't want to make known. This is well balanced deliverance!

This is the victory the new creation, the authority the new man has over the fallen angels. In Christ Jesus we are seated at God's right hand in authority and power. Just as Jesus commanded demons and said it is written to the fallen, so we are to do the same.

CHAPTER EIGHT

FALLEN ANGELS AND BELIEVERS AUTHORITY

Within the body of Christ, there seems to be this assumption, this belief and or action, that the believer has authority and power over the kingdom of darkness. Just because we have given something, doesn't mean that person knows how to operate in what Jesus has given. There seem to be a blind acceptance of a truth that can declare something without operating in certain realities, and without proof, power, and responsibility. Let me give you an example,

> *I have given you authority to trample on snakes and scorpions and to overcome all the power of the enemy; nothing will harm you. Luke 10:19 NIV*

Some translations like the King James Bible, mistranslate the word "authority" here as "power." Stating, "behold I give unto you power." Listen to what the King James says when you substitute the word power for authority. It says, "I have given you AUTHORITY to tread on serpents and scorpions, and over all the POWER of the enemy. It takes authority to overcome the enemy's power. So, the power the believer operates in reveals the authority of that believer over the kingdom of darkness.

In the Church's battle against the kingdom of darkness, and evil's authority to rule through sin, there is a hierarchy of fallen angels. There are demonic spirits who work for the fallen. One third of the angels fell, thus the name they identify themselves with or in deliverance sessions is fallen. They don't identify themselves as fallen angels, but fallen. They do not want humanity to know they are angels that fell. When the believer is operating in proper authority, the fallen must obey God's laws enforce by humanity.

These fallen angels have set up a kingdom as Jesus says in Matthew 12:25, and their mission or assignment is to overthrow God's government. The leader of God's government is Christ Jesus. Jesus' government comprises many cultures of people groups around the world over many spans of time since the resurrection.

The measure of authority within the Church rest on the power behind that authority. The reason we don't see more authority in the Church, the Church has not learned to move and grow in measures. With each measure we learn how to exercise authority through power that God has delegated within that measure. To tread on means to step on or to press the foot on. This is a reminder of the Genesis 3:15 account. We realize that God has design levels of authority to be achieved as we operate within those dimensions.

The Church is under some belief system that repentance for sin is all that is required. It also assumes that sanctification is yielding to the Holy Spirit for holiness of sinful behavior. These statements are true but incomplete. Repentance gives us entrance (salvation) into the Kingdom of God, and obedience to the Holy Spirit brings sanctification, yet there is a deeper realm that must be dealt with. In dealing with demonic spirits, curse breaking, inner healing and deliverance goes hand in hand with repentance. It also aids in completing the sanctification process. But when we talk about fallen angels in the celestial realms, we must include the corruption of the human genetic code that came through the fallen angels and their offspring, the Nephilim. I was introduced to this type of deliverance through a prophetess who attended my Church, when she said the Lord had spoken to her. I felt the Lord was in it, and as always, behind closed doors, I asked God to verify with power through private deliverance. I saw generational sickness cease, and many other amazing things like baldness terminated generationally, even parental character traits ended.

Let us look at Wikipedia's definition of DNA: it is short for deoxyribonucleic acid and is the molecule that contains the genetic code of organisms. DNA is in each cell in the organism and tells cells what proteins to make. Mostly, these proteins are enzymes. DNA is inherited by children from their parents. Therefore, children share traits with their parents, such as skin, hair and eye color. The DNA in a person is a combination of the DNA from each of their parents. I have seen this character trait acted out both physically, through the soul, and spiritually.

Just as sin entered the world and corrupted the universe in this fallen age, so sin through the fallen angels have corrupted man's DNA. As the Apostle Paul said in 2 Corinthians 12 that he was taken up to the third heaven, it stands to reason that there must be a first and second heaven to have a third. It would also stand to reason that sin corrupted the whole chemical makeup of humanity if sin entered this age! What I am saying is that evil spirits must come out of our DNA when expulsion is taking place. You may say, what has our DNA have to do with the believer's authority? Everything! In the promise of salvation, our spirits today are renewed, our mind is being transformed, and at Christ's return, our bodies will be imperishable or enduring forever. Sin changed our DNA to where we die, sickness lives in the DNA, even character traits or the desire to do evil. We call this the sinful nature or the Satanic principle. This all affects our faith.

What I'm suggesting is that the Church look deeper into the spirit realm and understand that there are rules that must be followed when exercising spiritual authority. If we don't follow these rules, the results we seek will not happen. Jesus stated, "I have been given all authority in heaven and on earth" (Matthew 28:18). He then commissioned His followers to make disciples with the authority He has given to us. Jesus completed His mission by claiming all authority. The Church who operates in authority will make disciples to the end of the age.

To fulfill that decree in Matthew 28, Jesus gave the Church the Holy Spirit to empower and transform the world. Most Churches have correct doctrine, but not correct practice of the scriptures. This happens when the supernatural is replaced for a self-righteous gospel. For the Church to have correct authority, it will have to return to Apostolic leadership.

What distinguishes apostles from the members of the body of Christ is their extraordinary authority. Apostles demonstrate true Apostolic authority over the kingdom of darkness, especially over fallen angels. We understand that it is the Holy Spirit who is functioning within and is the one who delegates authority to believers.

And He Himself gave some to be apostles, some prophets, some evangelists, and some pastors and teachers, for the equipping of the saints for the work of ministry, for the edifying of the body of Christ, till we all come to the unity of the faith and of the knowledge of the Son of God, to a perfect man, to the measure of the stature of the fullness of Christ; that we should no longer be children, tossed to and fro and carried about with every wind of doctrine, by the trickery of men, in

*the cunning craftiness of deceitful plotting, but,
speaking the truth in love, may grow up in all
things into Him who is the head—Christ—from
whom the whole body, joined and knit together by what every joint supplies, according to the
effective working by which every part does its
share, causes growth of the body for the edifying of itself in love. Ephesians 4:11-16 NKJV*

When I read commentaries on these scriptures, all of them leave out the supernatural. Yet each of the people in the Bible had some form of supernatural ministry. The Greek word 'apostello' means to send out and with something sent. Strong's says an apostle is officially commissioned by Christ with miraculous powers. Apostles are designed to be raised up with authority to operate in the heavenly regions. Apostles are equipped to speak from the heavenly realms and to operate with the things that take place in the heavens. Today's so called Apostles do not do this. Apostles are called to work with the angelic armies of God to defeat the fallen angels in the four dimensions of the second heaven.

THE NEED FOR REVELATION

It is not revelation or the nature of revelation that opens new realms of authority, faith, and freedom, but the one that is equipped. This is the Apostolic ministry, pioneering the work through authority and power. Bringing those things in heaven to earth. It is absolutely impossible for the Church to live and demonstrate the life of Christ without receiving through supernatural encounter revelation from God. Hosea 4:6 says, "My people are destroyed for lack of knowledge." Knowledge is facts, information that has been worked out skillfully by a person through experiences and education. These facts command the unseen world. The information gained is directly from the Lord through supernatural activity. This knowledge produces supernatural breakthrough from encounters. When the Lord told me years ago, that He would reveal the secrets of the kingdom of darkness to me, I did not understand. But as I yielded to the deliverance anointing, hungered and thirsted for more knowledge, God brought powerful demons forward. Then God brought down the fallen angels, now over 20 years of experience, I'm writing and reporting the work of the Holy Spirit. This is not my work, but the Holy Spirit's work, for He has taken over many of the ministry sessions with fallen angel encounters and showed me straight away how this process is to be accomplished.

The five-fold ministry is too fully equip and perfect the saints for works of service. That is why each one of these ministries is so important. They are so different in calling and assignment. The body of Christ is in need of being built up. This seems to be a construction term. A putting together of parts and materials over time. We incorporate and establish through development of a weaponized Church, ready to dismantle geographical fallen angels and the demons in their territory that work for them. An Apostle sees the importance of the five-fold ministry within their sphere of authority and seeks to build up, perfect, mature, and weaponize the Church. I use the word weaponize because it has two basic meanings. First, it is to supply and equip with weapons. Second, and I like this meaning, is to convert to use as a weapon. In dealing with fallen angels, demonic spirits of all kinds, I have had to weaponize the word of God to defeat the secret powers of darkness.

Proverbs 29:18 says, "Where there is no revelation, the people cast of restraint." If we reduce this scripture to prophetic revelation, we can only operate in part. Prophetic revelations are things that start to come to pass, and in the future come fully to pass.

Realms of the kingdom of darkness has always been revealed first, through a statement from God, like, "I will show you something you have never seen before." Hours later, I was in a deliverance session and an alter personality from 600 years ago came forward who was Scottish. The realms of evil had also informed me on how to conduct myself when encountering evil spirits. I have also been told that I could not touch them because they were armed, referring to the armor of Satan. Extracting information or listening to boasting evil spirits, we are discerning and fitting into the model of deliverance God has given you is wisdom. Let me say as I did in the last chapter, God makes spirits say things, it is our job to discern right (helpful/hints) or wrong (lies). If the information coming through evil spirits, most of the time, will be lies. But God decides to order evil spirits to speak helpful hints, and in so doing, it is my job to discern and use the word of God to further the ministry session or the realm.

I discovered the armor of Satan through a witchcraft spirit. The armor of Satan had been in the word of God since the time they wrote the gospels. This spirit said I could not touch him, and that ended up happening. I lacked revelation through scripture; I lacked the weapons I needed to expel witchcraft. He was occult in origin. I did not know this particular spirit needed to be spiritually disarmed (Luke 11). The supernatural comes through God's voice with a demonstration of power that is visibly seen. It also can come through evil spirits being ordered by God, but this will only come with partial truth. The devil in the garden twisted the truth, this is a good example.

The witchcraft spirit did not speak truth to me, he only revealed he was armed, and that was only a hint towards truth. It was my job to study the scriptures like a Berean (Acts 17:11). Twisted truth is deceptive, wanting the wrong outcome. But as a good soldier in the army of the Lord, I untwist the truth; it left me with a scripture, also with a revelation, and the power of manifestation. I always tell the one who talks about revelation, manifest it in power! Revelation is a vision of what is coming, but it is also the power of God in the now! I need the vision of the unseen realm, the second heaven fallen angel structure and orders that must be revealed in power by God.

> *When a strong man, fully armed, guards his*
> *own palace, his goods are in peace. But when a*
> *stronger than he comes upon him and overcomes*
> *him, he takes from him all his armor in which*
> *he trusted, and divides his spoils. He who is not*

with Me is against Me, and he who does not
gather with Me scatters. Luke 11:21-23 NKJV

When reading spiritual warfare material and I come across statements like, "a high-ranking demonic principality," I understand they are writing out of assumed revelation. What I mean is, presumption. An idea that is taken to be true, and often used as the basis or other ideas, but not a total reality. In the heavenly realms there are principalities, but the word demonic reveals a state of things that are not factual and do not exist. The word demonic expresses the terrestrial realm, where principality conveys the heavenly realms, celestial, or the second heaven.

All fallen angels are armed, the scripture confirms combat experiences. I understand that the armor of God is for fallen angels and not protection from demons. Will it protect from demons? Yes, but that is not the original design. Look closely at the word of God:

> *Put on the whole armor of God, that you*
> *may be able to stand against the wiles*
> *of the devil. Ephesians 6:11 NKJV*

In this scripture it directly reveals that the armor of God helps us stand against the schemes of the devil which is also a metaphor for the fallen angels. We define wiles as deceit, trickery, or the cunning arts of evil that lie in wait. What is Paul saying? It is the craftiness of a way of doing something deceptive, especially in a systematic way; it implies an orderly, logical arrangement, usually in steps. This only comes through the fallen angels, not demons. Paul says directly in verse 12, we wrestle against principalities and power, against world dominators if you will, in the heavenly realms. See why I said the word devil is a metaphor, and the armor is for the fallen.

Luke has given us a full-blown similitude to that of a well-armed lord of a castle. This comparison between the visible realm and the invisible realm is the key to the believers victory in defeating fallen angels or strongmen. A lord is someone having power, authority, or influence. He is a man of noble rank or high office master over his castle and his jurisdiction. The Bible says God is Lord over the heavens and the earth. God is also Lord over the heavenly armies. These lords have many evil spirits as soldiers under their command.

I understand that demons are called strongmen when doing terrestrial bodily deliverance. They have to earn the right to be called, but are not from a royal line. It is more of an honorary title if you will. There are many different demonic strongmen, and could have many demons under them, but they work directly for the fallen angel who is by biblical definition defined as strongmen. There will be many lords, each fallen angel in its order, until we reach Satan.

Fallen angels are angelic majesties who Luke pictures as strongmen. They are the first ones or preeminent ones. They are leaders, lords, chief princes, princes, kings, captains. They were the beginning of this evil fallen age and call themselves the authors of sin. But demons are biblically defined as evil supernatural disembodied spirits. We have learned that thrones, dominions, principalities, and powers are levels and sub-levels of strongmen in the heavenly realms.

The angelic realms, both evil and good, are very highly structured and well organized. They are set up as in the form of a kingdom. Angels have descending orders of authorities according to their class and created number. According to their jurisdiction or territory, there are different rulers and sub-rulers responsible for different areas of authority in the heavenly realms who rule over the earth. Biblical definers call the heavenly realms regions above the earth. It is defined as space or vaulted arches high over the earth from one horizon to another. It includes the sun, moon, constellation, and stars.

These castles Luke is speaking of are defined as spheres of darkness dominated by the absence of light and power. They are spheres of authority who influence in and for darkness controlling the minds of humanity according to the will of the evil fallen angel lord. Words used from the Lexicon in speaking about areas are the earth, geographical areas, regions, space, districts, inhabited area's, territories, places, urban areas and wilderness. Let me give a scriptural reference here, Luke 20:20. The goal was to trap Jesus to hand Him over to the control and authority of Pilate the governor. Behind every person in authority is an angel. How a person governs is whether it is God's angel or a fallen angel influencing the mind.

In Luke 20:20 and Jude 6, the invisible and visible, what is interesting is that authority has reference to the beginning or origin. It is a foundation and a source. The reference is to elementary principles or principalities in office. Pilate was the visible ruler as governor, but an evil principality had control of his governorship and his region of control. In Jude 6, the invisible fallen angels left places of authority and power in their dwelling place or castle.

Let us take the word begin in the Bible with its meaning of initiating an action through a process for a state of being. It involves time in the definition. Begin then has to do with a point of or in time at the beginning of a duration or time which something continues until it has come to full length. There is another definition for a beginning I must comment on. Beginning is also defined as an expert or master builder. Every fallen angel who comes into power is there to build his kingdom first. For example, we know that when Jesus comes back, this evil age will come to a close, and at the end of the Millennium (Rev.20:1-5) evil will be done away with forever. Jesus the master builder will do away with time and evil.

The Church who understands that this is a generational war until the end of the age, is the Church who overcomes. Understanding my opponent is just as important as how to defeat my opponent.

> *For our wrestling match is not against flesh and blood [contending only with physical opponents], not against persons with bodies, but*

against cosmic powers and or fallen angels who
rule with various areas and descending orders
of authority. Against world dominators of this
present darkness, against spiritual forces of
wickedness in the heavenlies. Ephesians 6:12

Paul is saying that we call these fallen angels majesties, dignitaries, and the first one I met in a power encounter, glorious ones. He called himself the glorious one, the 24th in creation or order from Satan. Today I would know him by his title, glorious one, as a throne, or ruling archangel or prince. Through the courtroom battle was over God's Word and obedience to God's Word, all who were there at the meeting who had Masonic Lodge roots were set free. When the fallen angel called the glorious one came down for judgment, his strength and power gripped everyone who had ancestral history to the lodge. He grabbed ahold of the minds of man with a controlling power to dominate the thoughts of those who had ancestral roots to the Masonic Lodge. As he spoke through one person, it affected everyone. The battle was over, "it is written." It was also over the Churches position in Christ Jesus. Once the accusations were answered according to the Word of God, the people's minds were freed and then the people started coughing up demons. This is the believers victory over the fallen angels.

We as trained soldiers in second heaven combat, because of our position in Christ Jesus, we are strong enough and capable for actions that dethrone principalities. The key is to possess the knowledge and training which bring about godly qualities required to wrestle with fallen angels over the right to govern. Jesus' Kingdom reigns through righteousness. As we live for sanctification and seek to be trained, we through prayer, power evangelism, power ministry, and the real preaching of the gospel, the Church begins or starts a process of wrestling with fallen angels over the minds of humanity.

Paul says we are to stand in the heavenly realm that is to take a position on the battlefield and operate out of that position. Therefore, Paul says we need the armor of God, for the protection against fallen angels. As David stood on that battlefield against Goliath, the visible reflecting the invisible, it was the Lord God who upheld David and who upholds us. Goliath was the champion over the Philistine army and so fallen angels over demonic spirits.

This wrestling or struggle until the end of the age between the Church and the fallen angels is God's design to unleash His multifaceted wisdom in all it countless aspects. It is to make God's power known through the revealing of mysteries to the angelic rulers and authorities in the heavenly places. This war is all about God's glory being made known.

As the Church fights against fallen angels, to grapple or if you will, a street brawl for the minds of man, this contest is to throw the other down, and which is decided when the victor can hold his opponent down. If the fallen win, this means to strip the Church of the many blessings, inheritance, presence, and power that belongs to her through salvation. People are lost, the Church is held down and unable to get up and receive God's outpouring in Christ. These rulers, chief's, princes, and magistrates as Vine's calls them, must be engaged correctly and defeated. It is the position of the Church as Jesus' body, to exercise Jesus' authority and power in this evil age. It is the will of God that the Church be a light in a dark place, a city on a hill or territorial refuge. Remember what I said earlier about darkness' rule in the absence of light. What the Church won't wrestle for, the light cannot shine in those dimensions. If it won't wrestle in prayer, the heavens cannot fully open. If the Church refuses to do power evangelism, mankind stays lost. If the Church will not contend for God's power, the blessings of God are few and far between.

Now the eleven disciples went to Galilee, to the mountain which Jesus had designated. And when they saw Him, they worshiped Him; but some doubted [that it was really He]. Jesus came up and said to them, "All authority (all power of absolute rule) in heaven and on earth has been given to Me. Go therefore and make disciples of all the nations [help the people to learn of Me, believe in Me, and obey My words], baptizing them in the name of the Father and of the Son and of the Holy Spirit, teaching them to observe everything that I have commanded you; and lo, I am with you always [remaining with you perpetually—regardless of circumstance, and on every occasion], even to the end of the age." Matthew 28:16-20 Amplified

CHAPTER NINE

FALLEN ANGEL POWER ENCOUNTERS

In my early days of doing spiritual warfare and power encounters, I could only look at scripture supernaturally and theologically as I understood it or experienced it. I believe this is true of all of us. I also don't claim that I understand everything related to all things in scripture. In this text of scripture, I have read it and taught it in part. In other words, I operated and taught Matthew 12 from an understanding of the demonic realm and from other writers. But today, I would like to pull back the veil, and open our minds to a dimension that is written here in scripture, but few understand it.

Then one was brought to Him who was demon-possessed, blind and mute; and He healed him, so that the blind and mute man both spoke and saw.

And all the multitudes were amazed and said, "Could this be the Son of David?" Now when the Pharisees heard it they said, "This fellow does not cast out demons except by Beelzebub, the ruler of the demons." But Jesus knew their thoughts, and said to them: "Every kingdom divided against itself is brought to desolation, and every city or house divided against itself will not stand.

If Satan casts out Satan, he is divided against himself. How then will his kingdom stand? And if I cast out demons by Beelzebub, by whom do your sons cast them out? Therefore they shall be your judges. But if I cast out demons by the Spirit of God, surely the kingdom of God has come upon you. Or how can one enter a strong man's house and plunder his goods, unless he first binds the strong man? And then he will plunder his house. Matthew 12:22-29 NKJV

Most commentaries are very brief in their comments on verse 22. Matthew tells us that this man had a demon, and the demons function or his assignment was to make the man blind and mute. From the beginning until now, my spiritual warfare training has continually revealed that there is never just one demon. My experience tells me that demons work in groups. Just as fallen angels work in groups. Demon possession happens through legal rights and or curses. Possession is in part, not in total. Parts of this man was tormented in his emotions. The man was able to free willingly choose to have them bring him to Jesus. This shows the man's will to be free. Many good willing saints bring loved family members for deliverance, yet that person deep down inside does not want to be free. If the will of man is not seeking, the supernatural does not happen in most cases.

The definition of possession here is to be under the power, control, and influence of a demon. Possession in the Bible has to do with affliction. Affliction is more than some hardship, adversity, or sorrow, this is included, but the hardship or pain is due to some disorder physically or in the soul due to a spiritual condition. The person is vexed or under a curse. Most legal rights have curses attached to them in possession. This Greek word possession is used thirteen times in the New Testament.

Matthew does not specifically label the healing an exorcism, but v. 24 assumes one has occurred. The man was blind and mute. He needed spiritual intervention, not healing. Possession infers the man was bound or tied as one with the demon, and those who work for the demon. Possession pictures being harnessed too. The point Matthew is making, the tying or harnessing to the demons is for security and safety. Luke tells us in chapter 11:21, a strong man is fully armed and guards his house so that his belongings are undisturbed and secure. The demon who's function was to cause the man to be blind and mute was secure due to his rights and curses to possess. Spiritually this man was imprisoned and held captive. There are other rights demons and fallen angels use to bring mankind into captivity. One is dissociation!

Dissociation is the separation and or disconnection from a state of being. People who have dissociative identity disorder or multiple personality disorder, have separated in the personality and thoughts to form another or more personalities due to trauma. In most cases, some form of abuse in childhood has transpired. When we hear the word abuse, we think of the worst, like physical, mental, or sexual abuse. Abuse can come about through not meeting the child's emotional needs. Let us use an example that happens often, but most would not see it as abuse. How about working so much that the child is cared for, but not emotionally. This is a form of abandonment and usually causes dissociation. To the well trained deliverance minister, we would know that demons are infested or immeshed into that persons emotions. We would also know, if demons are engrafted in the emotions, then fallen angels also have engrafted themselves in the mind of the person.

This brings us to the different fallen angel deliverances. More about this later, but I will comment here. One fallen angel could hold the full inheritance of the trauma, yet another could be over the family bloodline through iniquity. Thus the person would have to go through two fallen angel deliverances. One fallen angel deliverance for all that has happened within the traumatic time, and demon expulsion following after the fallen angel leaves. The second, for sins and curses committed in the bloodline within that generation or the generational trauma past down through the bloodline, with demon expulsion following after the fallen angel leaves. Since demons are the offspring of the fallen, it would be reasonable to see demons doing what the fallen angels have done before creation. Let me say it this way, demonic deliverance reveals fallen angel encounters, because demons work within the system of fallen angels. For more on this point, see my book on "Exploring Secrets of the Heavenly Realms." We also know that not every exorcism will be fallen. In most cases, the deliverance minister must take out enough demons to bring down the fallen angel.

This blind and mute man was to serve as a slave to the evil spirit. This is what vices or conditions reveal to us. Humanity being spiritually made slaves and brought into bondage to serve the function of evil spirits. It is the same for health issues, spirits of infirmity have enslaved the human body with the function of that infirmity. If it is some form of disease that needs to be managed or controlled or in remission by medicine or treatment, the spiritual man knows that it is an evil spirit of infirmity at work.

Let us look at a spirit of infirmity in Luke!

POWER ENCOUNTER IN LUKE

Now He was teaching in one of the synagogues on the Sabbath. And behold, there was a woman who had a spirit of infirmity eighteen years, and was bent over and could in no way raise herself up. But when Jesus saw her, He called her to Him and said to her, "Woman, you are loosed from your infirmity." And He laid His hands on her, and immediately she was made straight, and glorified God.

But the ruler of the synagogue answered with indignation, because Jesus had healed on the Sabbath; and he said to the crowd, "There are six days on which men ought to work; therefore come and be healed on them, and not on the Sabbath day."

The Lord then answered him and said, "Hypocrite! Does not each one of you on the Sabbath loose his ox or donkey from the stall, and lead it away to water it? So ought not this woman, being a daughter of Abraham, whom Satan has bound—think of it—for eighteen years, be loosed from this bond on the Sabbath?" And when He said these things, all His adversaries were put to shame; and all the multitude rejoiced for all the glorious things that were done by Him. Luke 13:10-17 NKJV

When I read commentaries and or author's on certain subjects, I have this inner thought of why would someone write something in which they have absolutely no spiritual training on the topic. What I mean is that one would write out of what they believe the Word of God says, instead of power encounter through the Word.

The woman was loosed, which means she was possessed. Remember the definition, possession infers the woman was bound or tied as one with the demon, and those who work for the demon. Possession pictures being harnessed too. Jesus says evil considers the human body as their house. Let me use another biblical definition that Strong's uses. The figurative meaning is to pardon or divorce. Pardon is the action of forgiving or being forgiven for an error or offense. This woman had to forgive anyone who had hurt her in any way. She also need forgiveness from Jesus. We do not read this is scripture, but the definition let us go deeper into the scriptural account. Being forgiven by Jesus and forgiving people are laws in the spirit realm that bring divorce from contractual agreements with evil made through unforgiveness and sins unconfessed. There is confession unto salvation, and that covers the spiritual and eternal part of mankind to be born again. There is another side to forgiveness, and that covers the believer in this fallen age or the flesh, and the freedom from the kingdom of darkness.

> *For if you forgive other people when they sin against*
> *you, your heavenly Father will also forgive you.*
> *But if you do not forgive others their sins, your*
> *Father will not forgive your sins. Mathew 6:14-15*

If we examine this scripture in light of the teachings of Jesus, these scriptures are talking about being forgiven in this evil age. We could say, be divorced and pardon from evil spirits which hold legal rights, curses, strongholds, oaths and vows, witchcraft covenants, blood curses, generational iniquities.

Jesus was doing the Father's work, He healed or delivered this woman on the sabbath. Jesus says something of vital importance, this woman satan had bound. Remember I said satan is used of himself or a metaphor for the fallen angels. Here then we see the fallen angel who actually owned the sickness, but the demon possession within the body was carrying out the function. My point is that the demon had second heaven protection. Jesus Himself said, satan had bound this woman. In my early days, I would have interpret this to mean, demon only possession. Today, with over one thousand second heaven fallen angel encounters, I know from experience that both the celestial and terrestrial realms must be dealt with. How I do this is, ask Jesus to stand in-between me, the person, and the second heaven. Then I deal with the demonic. Second, I ask God the Father to send down the fallen angel who holds the right to inflection, the bloodline with sickness, and ask God to judge him.

THE SAMARITAN POWER ENCOUNTER

Then Philip went down to the city of Samaria and preached Christ to them. And the multitudes with one accord heeded the things spoken by Philip, hearing and seeing the miracles which he did. For unclean spirits, crying with a loud voice, came out of many who were possessed; and many who were paralyzed and lame were healed. And there was great joy in that city. Acts 8:5-8 NKJV

The scripture tells us that the Samaritans first listened to Philip because of the miracles God was doing through Philip. In most cases, it is the power ministry that brings multitudes. This opens the doors to the message of the gospel, and it is the message what changes mindsets. Philip was doing what we call today, power evangelism. We see how the early Church responded to the Great Commission. The book of Acts reveals that the disciples went out and spread the good news with demonstrations of God's power. The key to any great revival is location and timing. God had gotten the Church ready to expand the kingdom. We see that Philip not only taught what the apostles instructed but also did what the Holy Spirit was moving in.

Today the Church is to continue the works and teaching of Jesus. The Great Commission is none other the ministry of Jesus done through His Church. We also can conclude from the scripture that the next generation of ministers was coming forth. Evangelism with God's blessing is more ministers bring forth Jesus' ministry. These second generation ministers were Stephen, Philip and Ananias. As the gospel spread throughout Asia Minor, we see the third generation of power ministers coming forth in Barnabas, Silas and Timothy.

The bible states that the first miracles done was deliverance from unclean spirits. These spirits cried out because of God's judgment against them. In corporate deliverance, I read a general renunciation and have the people repeat it as we go through it. Covered in this renunciation, is forgiveness of sins, legal rights, curse breaking, soul tie breaking, oaths, vows, and renouncing the kingdom of darkness and all evil spirits on the page. I also have them renounce the second heaven or fallen angels over their bloodline, territory, nation. When I say come out, God's power descends, and the Holy Spirit drives them out. The people start to cough, vomiting, screaming, evil spirits take the person over, and emotional trauma manifests. It is powerful, but messy! Ministry like this does not appear in your mama's Church. If I start with deliverance, I find the amount of healings that take place afterwards is at least 50% higher. If I drill down on spirits of infirmity after demonic deliverance that can reach up to 70% healed in one meeting.

Here is something else I find in operation. The Holy Spirit is exercising judgment against the kingdom of darkness, people just by faith got healed. They stand up out of wheelchairs because they see the manifestation of the Holy Spirit in the judgment against evil spirits. People would say I saw God's power against evil, sickness came through sin, so I got up in faith or I ask God in Jesus' name to heal me, and it happened.

It appears in scripture, if we take Philip's account, deliverance was God's first desired miracle, evil spirits crying aloud as they were expelled. As Philip followed the Holy Spirit, I have come to the same conclusion, there are many people who are possessed today. If anyone does corporate deliverance, one can become so busy that healing is not thought about until things calm down. I notice about 50% of the people who are set free are healed right there. The rights to the sickness have been forgiven, so the affliction or the possession, which ever pertains, is gone, so healing takes place.

Notice how God desires to grab mankind's attention; the people hearing the miracle realm through sounds of deliverance. They also heard people declaring their healing. The multitude also saw the evil spirits manifest and seeing the paralyzed and lame healed.

> *Now there was a man named Simon, who previously practiced magic in the city and amazed the people of Samaria, claiming to be someone great. They all paid [a great deal of] attention to him, from the least to the greatest, saying, "This man is what is called the Great Power of God!" hey were paying attention to him because for a long time he had mystified and dazzled them with his magic. But when they believed Philip as he preached the good news about the kingdom of God and the name of Jesus Christ, they were being baptized, both men and women. Even Simon believed [Philip's message of salvation]; and after being baptized, he continued on with Philip, and as he watched the attesting signs and great miracles taking place, he was constantly amazed. Act 8:9-13 Amplified*

When a Church or ministry is experiencing the outpouring of the Holy Spirit and there is tremendous fruit, the occult will usually show up or fallen angels come down to war for the minds of men. When the occult shows up, it is to either do curses or to report back to the coven. The occult also likes to befriend to divide the Church or ministry, this spiritually weakens the anointing and spirit realm for harvest. When the fallen angels come down, the thoughts of the people come under attack, trying to get the people to reject part or all that God is doing.

What happens next is unusual or rarely happens. Simon the sorcerer becomes saved and water baptized. He believed in the message of salvation and the power of Jesus' name. What is normal and most don't understand is that Simon could not receive the baptism of the Holy Spirit because he did not go through deliverance? I find many people who have witchcraft contracts in their bloodline, unable to receive the baptism of the Holy Spirit due to the curses that block the reception.

Then Peter and John laid their hands on them [one by one], and they received the Holy Spirit. Now when Simon saw that the Spirit was given through the laying on of the apostles' hands, he offered them money, saying, "Give me this authority and power too, so that anyone on whom I lay my hands may receive the Holy Spirit." But Peter said to him, "May your money be destroyed along with you, because you thought you could buy the [free] gift of God with money!

You have no part or share in this matter, because your heart (motive, purpose) is not right before God. So repent of this wickedness of yours, and pray to the Lord that, if possible, this thought of your heart may be forgiven you. For I see that you are provoked by bitterness and bound by sin." But Simon answered, "Pray to the Lord for me both of you, so that nothing of what you have said will come upon me." Acts 8:17-24 Amplified

Simon was acting like a baby Christian and a true occult member even though he received salvation by believing the gospel. Simon offered money for the baptism of the Holy Spirit. Members of the occult pay for the power of the devil. Psychic's charge money and witches due the same for the ceremony and rituals contained within the ceremony. The Church must remember that the anointing and the baptism of the Holy Spirit comes without cost. This will include the ministry gifts of the Holy Spirit. Ministers should not charge and the Church should not withhold money. One way the Church withholds money is through not tithing. Another way is not to support a private ministry. I see this happen often, people go to a specialized ministry like deliverance and want deliverance for free or little to nothing. Greed in the body of Christ is an enormous problem. I notice ministers charging especially for deliverance, this should not be so. I understand why they charge. People who come for deliverance hold back their money, not understanding that money is a contractual or binding transaction. Simon Magus understood the power of exchange.

Peter rebuked Simon and his offer to buy God's Spirit. Peter reveals something powerful by stating that Simons heart, motives, and purpose was wrong. Peter told him to repent of his wickedness and get delivered of evil. Simon was bond or under the control of evil through bitterness and sin. As I stated before, curses are binding, and travel from generation to generation until broken. Peter gives Simon the solution, pray to the Lord that, if possible, this thought of your heart may be forgiven you.

As stated in Chapter One, casting out evil spirits weakened the territorial fallen angel. The ruling territorial spirit along with the other fallen angels who work for him, by casting out demons, Philip was weakening the army in that territory. Ministries who operate in deliverance and healing shift the power struggle between light and darkness. When the atmosphere shifts through the casting out of evil spirits, other ministry gifts like the prophetic and healing become more powerful. When people receive the baptism of the Holy Spirit, atmospheres are shifting and prayer is one weapon God has armed the Church with. We can conclude that one of two things happens when power ministries cast out demons, the fallen angels come down or the occult sends a member.

We understand that when the gospel is not going forth as designed; it is because the god (fallen angels) of this age has blinded the minds of those, who do not believe. The gospel is the glory of Christ, who is the image of God. When mankind understands he needs a savior, convicted through the preached word, and gets saved, the light of God shines on him.

We know from scripture that the kingdom of darkness is a highly organized and well structured to keep mankind captive. The fallen angels who operate as officers and the demons who function as soldiers were not in disarray but under attack when power ministry is done. Through what some call ground-level strategic warfare, which is none other than casting out evil spirits, the battle for human souls was on. Some writers even suggest that the ground-level activity could have succeeded in greater ways if they had bound the strongman. When writers say things like this, I quickly realize they have never come face to face with a fallen angel. How do I know this? When people are repenting, being saved, breaking curses so that demons are coming out, being healed, receiving the Holy Spirit, this is binding the strongman. The fallen angel over that territory being bound from his work as the Holy Spirit is exercising authority and dominion through outpouring. The Church in most part does not see this revelation. But as I cast out demons, there will come a time when the fallen angels come down to defend their territory. These are the facts, and I have over one thousand second heaven encounters to support my hypothesis.

One particular author writes that demons aren't here to make mankind sin. He also says evil has more sinister things to do than make sock puppets out of people. Don't you believe it! The kingdom of darkness is sin and evil spirits influence mankind to sin, but we choose. Although fallen angels have thrones, dominions, principalities, and powers, their territorial jurisdiction, demons also have terrestrial levels. What makes evil spirits evil? The evil spirits level or rank and his wickedness has a direct influence by who fathered and how much he can accomplish through sin. Demons can move up the ladder so to speak as they accomplish their assignments by influencing sin; we can say, they receive promotion by the fallen angels within that region. Much like a persons height is determined by genetics and diet. This is also true with a person who has been takeover through demon possession. The demons within the host fight for control of the host so they move up the ladder inside. This also is a true hypothesis proven from thousands of exorcisms.

Bless the Lord, you His angels,
You mighty ones who do His commandments,
Obeying the voice of His word!
Bless the Lord, all you His hosts,
You who serve Him and do His will.
Bless the Lord, all you works of His, in all places of
His dominion;
Bless and affectionately praise the Lord, O my soul!
Psalm 103:20-22 AMP

This scripture is powerful and supernatural in effect. We see that all of God's angels are to bless Him. Those different classes of angels according to rank and number within the four dimensions, and God's divine counsel. God's angels are to praise Him and to speak words of excellence about Him. When I open my meetings with come Holy Spirit and when I praise God, speak about His wonders, the presence of the living God descends on the congregation in powerful ways. My point here is that angels are spoke of as a collective. Then the scripture communicates that these angels are to do His commandments (Word of God) and to obey God's voice. In second heaven fallen angel deliverance, God will give me scripture, and as I read the Word of God exactly as written in prayer form, the fallen angels lose rights. God also provides His second heaven angels in the deliverance session, and they preform the Word of God as the Church prays. God uses His angels in the deliverance session to serve His will, which is a shadow of what is coming. The Church as we approach the end time, will be more involved in second heaven warfare and will cause Michael and God's angels to war over the second heaven collectively, as described in Revelation 12:7-8. Remember what Paul wrote in Ephesians 3:10, that through the Church, the manifold wisdom of God should be make known to the rulers and authorities in the heavenly realms. Today, God is ready for both heaven and earth to join in His works and in all places of His dominion. Paul writes about this in Ephesians 1:11, that in Christ, God has make known to us the mystery (secrets revealed in proper time) of His will. At the fulfillment of times, the end of history, God in Christ, at the climax of this evil age, bringing all things together in Christ, both things in the heavens and things on the earth.

You may ask, what is an example of scripture you pray. In Colossians 2:13-15 the Amplified Bible says:

When you were dead in your sins and in the uncircumcision of your flesh (worldliness, manner of life), God made you alive together with Christ, having [freely] forgiven us all our sins, having canceled out the certificate of debt consisting of legal demands [which were in force] against us and which were hostile to us. And this certificate He has set aside and completely removed by nailing it to the cross. When He had disarmed the rulers and authorities [those supernatural forces of evil operating against us],

He made a public example of them [exhibiting them as captives in His triumphal procession], having triumphed over them through the cross.

Here is another powerful key and rule in the battle against the fallen angels in the second heaven. Again, when I mention the second heaven, I am talking about all four dimension. The fallen accuse humanity, both saved and unsaved, because of our condition in the flesh. The worldly lifestyle that exhibits behavior and thoughts. Unfortunately, humanity displays ungodly manners of the heart which allow the fallen angels to accuse. The fallen use documents (scrolls as they say) or certificates of debt, other object such as willful sin, and produce these items in God's courtroom.

Colossians 2 is what Christ Jesus has done for us positionally, but there is another side, the sinful condition that is being sanctified. This is as plain as day. Humanity has two natures, the nature of Christ for those who are born again, and the nature of the flesh or the satanic principle. The scriptural instruction here is to cancel out the sins and transgression done in the flesh. One must be very careful here not to confuse their position in Christ through forgiveness of sin, and their condition in the flesh because of sin. I am not naïve or obtuse to the doctrines of justification, sanctification, and glorification. When God the father sends the fallen angel and his tribe (they say) or council, I pray that they present their certificate of debt in God's court. As the fallen angel who speaks for the tribe reads the certificate of sins, the contractural agreements with them, binding the person to them, I rebut and counter through the Word of God, what Christ Jesus did for us on the cross. I agree God made us eternally alive in Christ Jesus and has forgiven us freely of all our sins. I argue in prayer form what is written through Christ Jesus. That God has canceled out every certificate of debt or the legal demands in force against us and hostile to us in the fleshly nature.

The scripture commands the Church to continue the process until every legal demand of debt is nailed to the cross. This is when God disarms the evil heavenly rulers called fallen angels. Once every sin has been judged by God in Christ Jesus, I then pray for the eternal chains of darkness, that thick gloom or total darkness to shackle them. This is an amazing thing to watch as the fallen angels scream, knowing God is sending them to tartaros. We find in Jude 6, and notice closely that the fallen angels who receive judgment in this evil age, God will not release after the millennium. They are chained in pits of gloom, imprisoned there for judgment as 2 Peter 2:4 says. The problem most scholars have with this scripture is that they don't operate in the supernatural. Scholars says God chained the most wicked fallen angels. Second Peter is a pronouncement by God for the Church to enforce. If God threw the angels that sinned into hell, as the scripture reads, then Satan and all the angels would also be there.

Ephesians 6:12 is talking about the fallen angels. Paul is saying that these second heaven fallen angels are the commanders, captains, the generals and the powers of darkness. If the fallen were all in chains, Paul has misspoken here. Paul has expressed scripture inaccurately. What Paul is driving at in Ephesians 6, fallen angels influence pagan and sinful culture. Paul is saying that the Church is to preach the gospel knowing the fallen angels within territories will stir up the minds and hearts of the unbelieving to withstand and drive out ministries.

I would not be serving you well if I did not mention Ephesians 2:1-3.

> *And you were dead in your trespasses and sins,*
> *2 in which you formerly walked according to*
> *the course of this world, according to the prince*
> *of the power of the air, of the spirit that is now*
> *working in the sons of disobedience. 3 Among*
> *them we too all formerly lived in the lusts of*
> *our flesh, indulging the desires of the flesh and*
> *of the mind, and were by nature children of*
> *wrath, even as the rest. Ephesians 2:1-3 NASB*

In Ephesians here, Paul is saying that we were (being) dead in trespasses and sins. The definition for 'were' is to possess certain characteristics, whether inherent or existing in something as permanent. The definition also means transitory or not permanent. What is Paul talking about? He is speaking about sin and trespasses forgiven through justification, sanctification, and glorification. Paul is identifying the two natures of mankind in this evil age. Paul is saying that there is a nature called the satanic principle inherent in humanity during this evil age. As I wrote in volume one of "Exploring Secrets of the Heavenly Realms," I did not like this finding. In one of my power encounters with Satan, he claimed possession of all mankind, saved or unsaved. I understand that the fallen are liars and father lies. I could sense from the Holy Spirit that there was something He wanted me to investigate. As I turned to scripture, I found as Paul here writes, through the sinful nature the fallen angels have access, that means something permanent. My hope came from Ephesians 4:22-24 where scripture instructs me to put off that sinful nature which comes through crucifying the flesh. To put on my new nature which was created in Christ Jesus. This means the Church can close doors if you will to the fallen angels and making sin transitory, not permanent.

When Paul uses the word course, and infers through his words he is talking about a throne, a lordship that rules in power through wickedness. Paul is talking about an archangel (Satan) throne who has supernatural power in controlling the destiny and activities of human beings throughout this evil age. We know Satan can't be everywhere, so Satan here is a metaphor for all archangels who have thrones around the world, and influence the minds of mankind to dominate times and destinies of nations. Paul reveals both the celestial and terrestrial realms in verse three. He says all mankind indulged in the flesh. This is a reference to the terrestrial realms where demonic activity on many levels take place. Paul also speaks of the indulgence or the satisfaction of the mind. This is referring to the celestial realm or the second heaven. Where Paul in Second Corinthians 4:4 says the god of this age, the fallen, have blinded the minds of unbelievers. As stated earlier in this book, Paul is talking about the unsaved, yet unbelief is the function of all fallen angels. As I mentioned before, through the sinful nature that affects the mind and body, the fallen have access or entrances to places within humanity.

WHY THE FALLEN MUST COME DOWN

The burning bush account recorded in Exodus 3:1-14 is a perfect example of God and an angel coming down in the manifestation of the burning bush. The Hebrew word 'angel' in verse 2 means messenger and root meaning to despatch as a deputy. So we can conclude that our text is referring to the invisible God and in some form, a visible angel. What made the ground holy? God's invisible presence. What made Moses afraid? God despatched an angel or messenger was for duty. This deputy was an angel whose immediate superior was present in an invisible form. From the definition I can conclude that the angel was of the highest legislatures, comprising the sovereign rule of God. From my past supernatural encounters I would surmise this was an angel of the princely realm. Some would ask, if God is doing the talking, why would an angel need to be there? The answer is simplistic for the supernatural person. It is only the theologians who make this a complex issue. The angel was there to hear the Word of the Lord and to aid Moses in the heavenly realms against the god's of Egypt. In supernatural warfare, angels inform or message angels; they are also there in surveillance functions; they also assist in warfare. When I started doing deliverance against fallen angels, God the Father assign three angels from the second heaven to stand guard over my life. These angels act as shields so that all classes of fallen angels can't touch my life.

"God, before whom my fathers Abraham and Isaac walked, the God who has fed me all my life long to this day, the Angel who has redeemed me from all evil, bless the lads; let my name be named upon them, and the name of my fathers Abraham and Isaac; and let them grow into a multitude in the midst of the earth." Genesis 48:15-16 NKJV

In Jacob's account it uses the same Hebrew word as in Moses' passage. God sent an angel to fight against all evil or territorial fallen angels who want to withstand the promises of God. In these passages the angel came down on God's demand. The angel was there to carry out God's blessings.

"Behold, I send an Angel before you to keep you in the way and to bring you into the place which I have prepared. Beware of Him and obey His voice; do not provoke Him, for He will not pardon your transgressions; for My name is in Him. But if you indeed obey His voice and do all that I speak, then I will be an enemy to your enemies and an adversary to your adversaries. For My Angel will go before you and bring you in to the Amorites and the Hittites and the Perizzites and the Canaanites and the Hivites and the Jebusites; and I will cut them off. Exodus 23:20-23 NKJV

God had ordered the angel as His representative to go before Moses and guard him on his journey. When God assigns angels, He assigns all those who work for them. I have been in second heaven deliverances with people who are living in open sin, and I am warned to have them removed from the session. As we see in the scripture, sin could not be among them, for God's name was in him. This brings me to a very important point. There are angels, both righteous and evil, that carry the name of Jesus. I pointed this out in my first volume of "Exploring Secrets of the Heavenly Realms." High level fallen angels take on the names of Jesus and exalted titles or words in scripture. Theologians make the mistake claiming this is Yahweh or God. They use the scripture, my name is in him or he will not forgive your transgressions. For example, the Bible calls Satan an angel of light or transforms himself into an angel of light. The Bible also calls Jesus the light of the world.

Before we move on to the next chapter and territorial spirits, let me give an example that will shed light on the situation. Let us pick a name that most believers are familiar with in the second heaven. A fallen angel who is a principality. What is the definition of a principality? Principalities are "first ones, preeminent ones, leaders,"- it means beginning, chief in order, time, place or rank; old or ancient; author, captain, prince. I can't get into this much, but look closely at when God created them, before Adam. Not only is this definition true, but in spiritual warfare through countless power encounters, they have confirmed the definition. Notice something else, their rankings like a captain or prince. Daniel even calls them kings. But when we look at definitions of demons, the Bible defines them as evil supernatural beings or evil spirits who are agents of evil to harm, bring distress, and ruin. No rulership definition. Nothing concerning their order in the creation and nothing about the authorship.

For by Him all things were created that are in heaven and that are on earth, visible and invisible, whether thrones or dominions or principalities or powers. All things were created through Him and for Him. And He is before all things, and in Him all things consist. Colossians 1:16-17 (NKJV).

In each of these levels of power, there are different rulers and sub-rulers worldwide. In each of these levels of the fallen, these spheres of jurisdiction, in the second heaven, each of these rulers or fallen angelic majesties have a creative order. It is actually a number they use which as a ranking! This determines where Satan and his ruling counsel has assigned them. There are as I know it today, nine different classes of fallen angels on all four levels of thrones, dominions, principalities, and powers. Here are contrasting names from 13 different translations of what the bible calls the fallen angels: glorious ones, glorious beings, angelic beings or majesties, celestial beings, dignitaries (glorious ones), supernatural beings, or those in exalted positions. Remember, I said Paul calls the devil an angel of light. Paul directs us to the interaction of heaven and earth, what is in the heavens affecting what is happening in the earth. Fallen angels through the willful sin of mankind can come and go from the heavenly realms to the earthly realms.

Chapter Ten

Territorial Fallen Angels

A s I begin our subject on territorial spirits or fallen angels with geographical authority, we must go back to the beginning or what I call the foundation scripture that opens wide the spirit realm.

> *For we do not wrestle against flesh and blood, but against principalities, against powers, against the rulers of the darkness of this age, against spiritual hosts of wickedness in the heavenly places. Ephesians 6:12*

My Translation of Ephesians 6:12: For our wrestling match is not against flesh and blood [contending only with physical opponents], not against persons with bodies, but against cosmic powers and or fallen angels who rule with various areas and descending orders of authority. Against world dominators of this present darkness, against spiritual forces of wickedness in the heavenlies.

This pictures a very highly structured and well organized kingdom with fallen angels and demonic spirits who have descending orders of authorities and different rulers and sub rulers responsible for different areas of authority in the second heaven and on earth.

Paul is telling the Church that to have success regionally or nationally, the Church will have to engage as the definition states, to engage in close hand to hand combat. The question then is how does the Church do this? We learn that our weapons for spiritual warfare are spiritual weapons. This opening may sound like principles written about earlier in this book, but indulge me to go deeper.

PRAYER AS A WEAPON

Paul tells the Ephesian Church that prayer is the central component to defeating territorial fallen angels. Without prayer, there can be no hand to hand combat. The Church majority must be involved, not just a few that attend regularly scheduled prayer meetings. Territorial fallen angels have four dimensions over every city, and many sub-levels in various areas of the city. These spiritual forces of wickedness seek to dominate the minds of mankind so that the city will not fulfill the destiny and purpose God foresaw.

Because of this, prayer meetings must reach levels of maturity where travailing intercession is taking place. Intercessor's who have the gift of impartation for intercession must be in attendance. These intercessors can pray for long periods of time and have the hunger to spend hours in daily prayer on their own. Those who attend the prayer meeting must understand that it is God's presence that must show up, and love for that presence a must. Waiting on God's presence, soaking in God's presence until the core group or the leaders feel it is time to pray. Some will travail in the beginning, others will pray in tongues.

The intercessory group must feel the burden of the Holy Spirit for the city and pray through. Praying through is praying until the burden lifts and in a lot of cases, holy laughter or joy breaks out. These intercessors stand on the front lines and beside Jesus as spiritual warfare prayer is taking place. They feel the protection of the Holy Spirit as He moves through them and follows Him into battle.

FALLEN ANGEL TERRITORIES

The work of fallen angels is to twist and distort through perverted mindsets, calling good evil and evil good. We understand that God allows Satan, and the fallen angels to exist and operate in this fallen age. We also must understand that God has dominion over all His creation. God also keeps the right to judge the fallen angels or the heavenly realms. I want to say it this way, God is the one who decides when to judge the fallen angels over cities. Yet, in the terrestrial realm, God has given mankind the right and authority to exercise dominion over demonic spirits. As I have said before and reiterate through the series, if the Church does not engage is spiritual warfare, that is casting out of demons, there will be no judgment of fallen angels within that territory.

Again, spiritual forces of wickedness seek to dominate the minds of mankind so that the city and the people will not fulfill the destiny and purpose God foresaw.

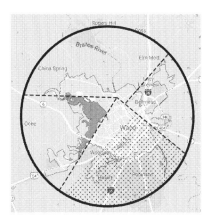

Now let's look at a principality that I faced getting a believer free from his rule. Here is a picture of one territorial fallen angel's dominion with sub-ruling fallen angels who have shared rulership, each responsible for their territory. Bible definitions call this a region. The Bible defines a region as a space lying between two limits or a tract of land; the (rural) region surrounding a city or village, the country. There is one principality or fallen angel over this city and his jurisdiction is shown by the outside circle. This fallen principality has sub-ruling principalities visible by the dashed lines. The dotted region shows the lower realms of darkness called powers!

The Bible defines darkness as the sphere dominated by evil, sinfulness, and ignorance of God and His ways; described as the absence of light. Now, I am about to reveal something very powerful. A sphere is a round solid figure, with every point on its surface equidistant from its centre. This means there is a fallen principality centered within that sphere. I would say by the lay of the land, the Masonic Lodge is Waco Texas' stronghold. The seat or rulership of that fallen principality. My Logos Bible Software program says, a sphere has each of a series of revolving concentrically arranged spherical shells in which celestial bodies were formerly thought to be set in a fixed relationship.

This fallen principality has covenant rights to the land, water, and the people who willfully sin within his territory. The ruling fallen principality calls those sub-ruling fallen angels his tribe or clan. They together rule over that sphere with authority, influencing darkness to stay in control of that realm and sub-realms. One of their biggest weapons is demonization. You see in the picture evil realms controlled by different levels of fallen angels. Paul tells us in Romans 13:12 AMP, "The night [this present evil age] is almost gone and the day [of Christ's return] is almost here. So let us fling away the works of darkness and put on the [full] armor of light." God will send someone who has the training to deliver regions, but most leaders have never faced down a principality, much less equipped to handle that kind of spiritual warfare. For example, when God sent me to Waco, many people who attended Waco Christian Center was sensitive to the Holy Spirit, yet I had to cast devils out of them all. This should not be! My point is the power ministries known as healing ministries do not deal with demons and fallen angels.

We know from Jude 6 that a fallen angels sphere of authority is over environments which people groups set up and live, so the fallen exercise a controlling influence, but mankind choses to establish surrounding conditions.

In the founding of Waco Texas, from the beginning, a ruling fallen angel over Texas (a throne/mighty one) called for or assigned a principality. The Lexicon says, from the beginning! This means, from the corner point or start point of Waco, an ancient ruler or fallen angel sought legal right. The job of the fallen principality was to set up institutions within his sphere so that sub-ruling principalities may move in. From there the kingdom of darkness sought to establish the business of sin so that second heaven fallen angelic powers would have rights to the land. The picture above uncovers one ruling principality with sub-rulers, yet the short lines reveal the lowest class of fallen angels called powers. Fallen angelic powers control zip codes as I found out in Waco. The fallen angels who go by the name powers are assigned sinful business' and establishments of sin so they can build their demonic army. This establishes their rule within that jurisdiction or zip code. So we must ask ourselves where are the troubled neighborhoods? We remember that fallen angels are military leaders. They have demonic troops assigned to them according to their angelic number. Yes, all fallen angels have classes and numbers. As mankind transgressed, principalities assigned demons to strengthen the fallen angels regional rights over the land. Principalities, we may call captains, over cities have many powers who we could call Lieutenant's and so sets up strongholds upon strongholds. Each fallen angel power who we are calling Lieutenant's have a stronghold. Like the military structure, Captain's have many Lieutenant's working for them.

We can see fallen angelic powers work in business, education, social groups, Churches, banks, city government, strip clubs, selling alcohol, drugs, all according to the ruling will of the territorial principalities over Waco. I use Waco as an example because this is where it all started for me. You may say Churches, yes, Churches. They have bewitched any Church that is not fulfilling Jesus' last order; they have come under the spell of the ruling fallen angels within that region. We must take heed to what the Apostle Paul is talking about in Romans 13:12. Jesus has asked the Church to preach, save, disciple, heal, and deliver, does your Church manifest these signs consistently? If not, your Church has come under the spell and will of the fallen principality of that region. You do not have to agree, but that doesn't make it not so.

When the Most High gave to the nations their inheritance, when he divided mankind, he fixed the borders of the peoples according to the number of the sons of God. Deuteronomy 32:8 ESV

Let us look at this picture on a bigger scale, in Dallas/Fort Worth where I live. There are approximately 2.6 million people who live in Dallas County and almost 1 million people who live in Fort Worth. Arlington Texas is in between Dallas and Ft. Worth, the population is about 400 thousand. There is one ruling throne over each city mentioned, but since Dallas has a higher population, he is the ruling fallen angel in the territory, but not the region. There would be many thrones under his command called the fallen angel counsel, and each city has a council. Each of these thrones who the Bible calls glorious ones, would have dominions under them which the Bible calls majesties or dignitaries. I have said before, each fallen angel has a number according to their creation order. Like Waco, there are principalities who rule under dominions and thrones, but that picture above was first shown to reveal a smaller area. Are you confused yet? I was when I first encountered them. There is one ruling throne over the region of Dallas/Ft. Worth, with sub-ruling thrones over each

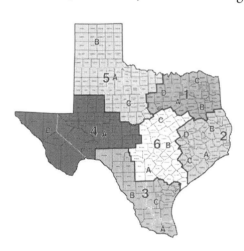

city. When we look at the state map, we see 6 regions and one state. We know that each fallen angel has a sphere, so these sphere's overlap, and that is according to definition as stated above. Remember when I quoted the Logos Bible Software on concentrical arranged sphere's. Concentric has to do with circles, arcs, or other shapes which share the same center, the larger often surrounding the smaller. The territories within the territories have celestial bodies or fallen angels and the people and land are in a relationship with them through sin. Many smaller circles or shapes within medium circles or shapes, and many medium circles or shapes within larger circles or shapes. This picture shows what is hard to explain. There is one ruling throne over Texas, and according to the population of man, many sub-ruling thrones within his sphere. The Bible translates all fallen angels as glorious ones, glorious beings, angelic beings, majesties, celestial beings, dignitaries in exalted positions. In the picture, we see overlapping spheres, I call them groups or tribes, each interwoven

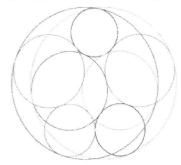

so that one would not be targeted and judged. Each of these fallen angels have numbers according to their classification and rank. The bigger the sphere, the higher the class and rank.

We can see a very highly structured organization of levels (spheres within spheres overlapping and intersecting) and each sphere has grades or rankings according to numbers within a hierarchy of each sphere.

This is a well-organized kingdom of four different dimensions all arranged in layers within the second heaven. These different fallen angels within each of the four dimensions have descending orders of authorities and different rulers and sub-rulers according to their grade and number within each sphere. These groups of fallen angels manage different areas of authority in the second heaven and rule over the earth through the minds of mankind. The strength and power of each sphere is the visible manifestation of sins controlling power to govern mankind's mind and behavior. Since fallen angels are first ones or preeminent ones, leaders according to Biblical definition, that would describe their function from the beginning as an expert or master builders. The Apostle Paul says in Ephesians 6:10-11:

> *In conclusion, be strong in the Lord [draw your strength from Him and be empowered through your union with Him] and in the power of His [boundless] might. Put on the full armor of God [for His precepts are like the splendid armor of a heavily-armed soldier], so that you may be able to [successfully] stand up against all the schemes and the strategies and the deceits of the devil.*

We are to be strong and draw our strength from Christ Jesus who empowers us. This is speaking about being capable for service through action as Jesus was. We are to act through the power of the Holy Spirit to control and bring dominion through the Church God's visible Kingdom shown through governing. Any army can defeat their enemy as long as they are equipped and well trained. Only well trained Churches and leaders can successfully bring victory over fallen angels as they deal with each realm according to the rules. If there is a geographical fallen angel, then people within the state, region, county, or city must repent and be in one accord. This starts as Churches come together to see mankind saved. Mass prayer groups must start up within the region and pray according to the rules. If not, we open ourselves up to an onslaught of destructive power from the ruling fallen angels within that territory. To not respect who they are in the creation and the power and authority God gave them before they fell is a big mistake.

Avoiding Second Heaven Problems

We can learn and make good decisions by how people write or speak about the second heaven. For example, those who write or talk about demonic principalities reveal their lack of knowledge concerning fallen angels. We should quickly avoid or be cautious in what is being said so we don't create potential spiritual problems. I like to caution believers because even Satan used the authority God had given him incorrectly and sinned. This led to their judgment and down fall. Operating mistakenly is in the eyes of fallen angels, disobedience to the Word of God and rebellion. We must stay away from false teachers that believe we can bind fallen angels over families, people groups, churches, geographical regions, states or nations.

When people have personal views, trouble is waiting to happen. The idea without power encounter has its origin in presumption. Their personal revelation is only a vain imagination and offers false hope unless God's power comes down, the territorial fallen angel speaks through someone of God's choosing, everyone falls out under evils power and the territorial fallen angel renounces the group and everyone gets delivered. Some cannot comprehend that fallen angels look at mankind as one. Ethic groups and geographical groups as an entirety, all depending on which fallen angel God is judging. In dealing with families, fallen angels over a family consider them as one. Demons target individuals and their offspring. Therefore, the Apostle Paul writes to the Corinthian Church, there should be no divisions among you. This means that each Church should be of one mind and one body, acting as the Lord Christ Jesus.

To the untrained soldier, the fallen will give small victories to lead you astray so to inflict harm. This could be financial, heath, children or the like. What I am talking about is that the untrained soldier goes off into his own imagination and this is vanity.

Let us not be obtuse in our thinking, for if we do not have a great understanding and power over demons, what makes us think the fathers or sires of the demons will obey. I am talking about the fallen angels. I have never tried to confront or call down a fallen angel, but have asked God if there is a fallen angel He would like to judge. I have a hard time thinking someone would have the audacity to bind or command a fallen angel in Jesus' name. The one who does things like this shows how little knowledge and power they really have. They also open their family line to rights that would require repentance. That would be the repentance of slandering angelic majesties.

Here is another vain imagination that has taken root in the body of Christ that one could go into the court of heaven as not to have a court case. That revelatory repentance covers all. What nonsense! This to reveals ignorance of the second heaven. There is always a court case, and the plaintiff and defendant must present their cases before God.

BEFORE GOD MADE THE WORLD

There are two things that at times I think mankind forgets, that God has always been and that the heavenly host was with God before the creation.

> *"Where were you when I laid the foundation of the earth? Tell Me, if you know and have understanding. "Who determined the measurements [of the earth], if you know? Or who stretched the [measuring] line on it? "On what were its foundations fastened? Or who laid its cornerstone, when the morning stars sang together and all the sons of God (angels) shouted for joy? Job 38:4-7*

When God was creating the world, the morning stars or the sons of God were there, shouting for joy. The Bible states that when God was laying the earth's foundation the angels were present. The Hebrew word foundation means to found, fix, establish, lay a foundation, it also the means to establish a base for construction. The fallen angels will brag about being the "first ones or preeminent ones" as the definition states. What they are saying is this, we were there in the beginning and so that makes us chief or first in the order of creation. Being there when God created the earth and man, the fallen angels remind and act like they are surpassing or without an equal and highly distinguished by order. In ministry sessions this is so clear. The fallen angels look at mankind as inferior, lower in rank, status or of lower quality and lower in position. Because mankind was made a little lower than the angels in this evil age, the fallen look at us in disgust. The fallen angels express a loathing

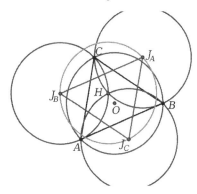

and outrage toward man and seen the higher up the fallen angelic order we go. The morning stars look at our intelligence and laugh. So those that just read about avoiding second heaven problems, take this as wisdom. As we look at the pictures it is my hope that all can see the complexity of the territorial organization as Paul states in Ephesians 6:12.

The naming by the word "host" draws on the description of celestial bodies and classifications in the heavenly realms. It directly points too many different classes and orders of the angelic realm, both of good and evil. It also speaks of vast multitudes of warriors and divisions who are well trained for combat and battle ready. In the U.S. Marine Corps there are three main infantry divisions. For example, the first marine division structure is organized by four regiments. Breaking this down a little further, there are four battalions to one regiment and four companies to one battalion. In most cases, there will be a major general or a two-star general as commander of a base. There is a colonel normally in charge of headquarters and battalions commanded by lieutenant colonels. This ranking structure runs down through the military until it reaches the platoon lieutenant. I find this structure very similar to the fallen angel orders or ranks and the armies who work for them. What I mean is that lower ranking fallen angels from thrones down to dominions, to principalities, to powers, to the infantry of demonic spirits of all classes. This is how the kingdom of darkness structure is laid out.

From our pictures we can see in the unseen realm a hierarchy of fallen divine beings with different levels of authority, responsibilities and jurisdictions. Job tells us, right from the start, God has divisions of angels all over the earth. Since that is so, then, Satan's structure is also the same. As we look globally, we now can see the amazing battle that awaits the Church.

This global layered authority is an administration set on destroying God's creation. This is why Jesus said that Satan and the fallen angels have come to steal, kill, and destroy. In 2 Peter 2:10, he speaks of angelic majesties, but the Bible also speaks of them as heavenly ones or glorious ones.

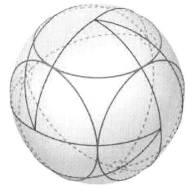

My first encounter with a fallen angel, his name was the glorious one. He was the 24 angel created after Satan. The assignment of the Church is global, no one minister can handle this massive call to take the gospel around the world and to defeat the fallen angels.

The fallen angelic majesties around the world are supernaturally powerful and are set on destroying this plant. The definition hints to a starting point, from territories or regions, to countries and then the earth. Isaiah 37:18 says the king of Assyria has devastated all their countries and their lands. When Isaiah says the earth will be completely laid waste, he likens it to a withering vine. One of the ways we can see mankind's problem to a shriveling plant is humanities poor health. In the supernatural, anything that resembles degeneration in any form is a sign of a curse.

The earth shall be utterly empty and utterly plundered; for the Lord has spoken this word. The earth mourns and withers; the world languishes and withers; the highest people of the earth languish. The earth lies defiled under its inhabitants; for they have transgressed the laws, violated the statutes, broken the everlasting covenant. Therefore a curse devours the earth, and its inhabitants suffer for their ; therefore the inhabitants of the earth are scorched, and few men are left. Isaiah 24:4-6 ESV

A curse is to cause injury or harm through a statement regarded as having supernatural power, often because they have invoked a deity or fallen angel, a supernatural force like a demon. A curse is a malediction and in ancient thought, the spoken word had intrinsic power and or the act of an utterance released intrinsic power. They exposed the person cursed to a sphere of destructive power. It worked effectively against a person until the power of the curse was broken. Isaiah says that a curse devours the earth. Why?

Because people of the earth have transgressed God's laws, violated the ways in which God has designed mankind to live by. Man has turned his back on God, and in so doing broken the everlasting covenant, God's covenant of man being his family. The question now remains, how does one defeat a fallen angel in combat. Psalm 82 is our answer.

PSALM 82 EXPLAINED

God stands in the congregation of the mighty;
He judges among the gods.
How long will you judge unjustly,
And show partiality to the wicked? Selah
Defend the poor and fatherless;
Do justice to the afflicted and needy.
Deliver the poor and needy;
Free them from the hand of the wicked.
They do not know, nor do they understand;
They walk about in darkness;
All the foundations of the earth are unstable.
I said, "You are gods,
And all of you are children of the Most High.
But you shall die like men,
And fall like one of the princes."
Arise, O God, judge the earth;
For You shall inherit all nations.

The original Hebrew word translated "gods" is elohim, and it refers to any inhabitant of the spirit world. Elohim does not refer to a specific set of abilities but distinguishes God from all other spirit beings. For example, Psalm 29:1

says, "Ascribe to the Lord, O heavenly beings, ascribe to the Lord glory and strength." The gods are commanded to worship God their creator as Psalm 148:1-5 speaks of.

When we examine verse one, it refers to the stance taken by a supreme ruler to receive the acknowledgment of his lordship in his court, and to address the accused by stating charges and to pronounce sentence. To stand means to attend or officially manage and to sort out. The God of the Bible is officiating a court case. He is there to oppose His enemies and to bring the fallen angels to court for wrong doing. We can see that it is God who judges the fallen angels.

The question how long in verse two does not seek an answer, however, but introduces a complaint and a demand that the offending activities sanctioned. The person who has the approval to operate in God's courts, appears in prayer and humility and pleads his case that the lawlessness of the fallen angels stop, cease immediately. In today's language, the person who God has appointed to operate in His court is to lead people in a declaration prayer. This criminal court proceeding concerns two things. One, the sins mankind has committed within that territory from the beginning and second, the lawlessness of the kingdom of darkness in that region. Asaph calls for both an indictment and a command that the gods cease judging unjustly. To judge in the spirit realm for the wicked.

These angels at one time represented God and held different level judgeships. Now Asaph is prayerfully asking that God recall their commission and to remove them from their magistrate. The prayer is for God to review these officers who judge over nations and who were to administer the law of God.

Within each region, whether a nation, state, county, city or zip code, Asaph is saying that we are to bring a court case against the fallen angels jurisdiction for their continual approval of injustice. In volume one of "Exploring Secrets of the Heavenly Realms", the chapter on territorial spirits, we must find out if this is a civil or criminal trial. If the trial is criminal, then officiated and judged according to the sins in our bloodline, and the sins of the population within that district. If the trial is civil, the court case will be personal sins and bloodline transgressions.

This is a powerful prayer and a major revelation for God's people. God actively desires to intervene in the interest of powerless people who cannot defend their rights because of the sin nature. As I have written before, the sin nature is the satanic principle. The sinful nature of humanity is the foundation and the system in which the fallen angels accuse and operate in mankind. Because this nature is of Satan, our belief's, attitudes, and behavior desire control. Therefore, a stronghold exhibits itself in three parts. The Bible teaches that every lie forms a stronghold foundation. Second, that lie calls for a chain of reasonings which then caps off the stronghold by thoughts that try to convince.

The fallen angels are to be brought to court because they have failed to act on behalf of the needy and weak. They have weakened mankind and in need of help because of the sinful nature. Asaph's prayer is for God to do justice by delivering mankind who seeks Him. Man is like a child who does not have a father to teach and guide. Asaph states in verse four for God to rescue man out of the hand of the fallen angels.

This is a formal charge by God in verse five of the gods, the fallen angel's true character as the verse describes. There disobedience to the sovereign Lord has caused them to act foolishly. Asaph used the word darkness or falsity to described their knowledge. The fallen angels walking about is the territory they oversee and influence evil. God says it is impossible for such gods or fallen angels to know, understand, have the ability, to see what is right.

When injustice and perversity have their way in the world, it shakes the spiritual and moral world order and comes under the threat of collapse. The Psalm points too, if the gods had their way, they would destroy the universe in a short time.

God said, you are gods [since you judge on My behalf, as My representatives]; indeed, all of you are children of the Most High, but you shall die as men and fall as one of the princes. To fall as one of the princes is to fall like mankind and to die for it. The beginning of the judgment finishes this powerful Psalm. The judgement against the fallen is because they have violated their purpose and mission to which God called them. But now God is judging them for their stupidity and rebellion. This is a powerful thing to watch, as they are chained with eternal chains of darkness and sentenced to tartaros.

As the series progress, it is my intention to bring out more Biblical revelations on the fallen angels. I hope and pray this series of books is a blessing and prepares the body of Christ for the showdown between the Church and the fallen angels.

Corporate Renunciation For Demons

Father God, in the name of Jesus, I ask you to forgive every sin I have committed, and every generational sin all the way back to Adam and the consequences of those sins. I now forgive all who have sinned against me and past generations, that have brought hurt and destruction. I break every curse I have created and every generational curse my ancestors have created and their consequences, I ask for your forgiveness God. Father, for every sin, transgression, and iniquity I ask for forgiveness and apply and accept the blood of Jesus to cleanse me and all generations walking the earth and all future generations.

I renounce every form of sickness, disease and infirmity and the sins, transgressions, and iniquities that brought them into my life, even past and current generations. I apply the blood of Christ Jesus and accept His atoning sacrifice for my healing. I renounce the life behind every sickness, disease and infirmity and ask you, God, to drive it out.

I renounce all forms of the occult and/or other religions. I renounce divination and sorcery and the nine covenants of the occult. I renounce their ceremonies, rituals, blood rights, soul ties, all forms of covenants, spells, oaths, pledges, incantations, pacts, initiations, and memberships. Every contract to the kingdom of darkness that I or my ancestors made, I now renounce and break them.

Father, if I or any ancestor gave their soul to the devil, I now renounce that and ask for forgiveness. I break any covenant, pact, blood right, pledge, or oath. I renounce the devil as god and confess that Jesus Christ is Lord to the Glory of God.

Father, in the name of Jesus, I now ask You for every generational blessing due to me from the foundation of the world, and every anointing, ministry gift, character gift, talent, and gifting. I now speak this renunciation and prayer over every generation walking the earth and every future generation to come.

Father, right now, in the name of Jesus, I now command, in the name of Jesus and by the power of Jesus' blood, that every evil spirit, demon, infirmity and familiar spirit leave me by coming out of my soul and body and every part of me, all the generations walking the earth and all future generations, our DNA, chemical body makeup and our bloodlines.

I now thank and praise the Father of all creation for my salvation, healing, deliverance, and freedom from curses and poverty in Christ Jesus. I thank you, Father, for restoring me to my full inheritance in Christ Jesus.

CORPORATE RENUNCIATION FOR FALLEN ANGELS

Father God, in the name of Jesus, I ask you to forgive every sin I have committed, and every generational sin all the way back to Adam and the consequences of those sins. I now forgive all who have sinned against me and past generations, that have brought hurt and destruction to my family bloodline. I break every curse I have created and every generational curse my ancestors have created and their consequences, and I ask for forgiveness Father God.

Father, for every sin, transgression, iniquity, and abomination in my family bloodline, I ask for forgiveness and apply and accept the blood of Jesus to cleanse me and all generations walking the earth, and all future generations. All sin, transgression, iniquity, and abomination that brought covenant, contracts, packs, or agreements with fallen angels I repent, I renounce them, I break all curses of evil including blood curses with the fallen angels. I apply the blood of Jesus to speak in your courtroom for me and my future generations and accept Jesus' atonement.

I renounce every form of sickness, disease and infirmity and the sins, transgressions, and iniquities that brought them into my life, even past and current generations. I renounce all legal rights, strongholds, curses that brought right for the fallen angels to hold as treasure all forms of sickness. I apply the blood of Christ Jesus and accept His atoning sacrifice for my healing in the courts of heaven. I renounce the fallen angels behind every sickness, disease and infirmity and ask you God to judge based on Jesus' cross.

I renounce all forms of the occult and/or other religions which gave right to fallen angels over my bloodline. I renounce divination and sorcery and the nine covenants of the occult and the powers of the fallen angels in this evil age. I renounce the fallen angelic ceremonies, rituals, blood rights, soul ties, all forms of covenants, spells, oaths, pledges, incantations, pacts, initiations, and memberships. Every contract to the kingdom of darkness and fallen angels that I or my ancestors made, I now renounce and break them based on Jesus' blood on the cross.

Father, if I or any ancestor gave their soul to the devil and fallen angels, I now renounce that and ask for forgiveness. I break that covenant, pact, blood right, pledge, and oath. I renounce the devil as god and confess that Jesus Christ is Lord to the Glory of God. I now ask for Jesus' blood to speak for me and acquit me of every certificate of debt that the fallen angels hold over my bloodline.

Father, in the name of Jesus, I now ask You for every generational blessing due to me from the foundation of the world in Christ Jesus. Every anointing, ministry gift, character gift, talent, and gifting that is due me in Christ Jesus. I now speak this renunciation and prayer over every generation walking the earth and every future generation to come and ask you Father God to render judgment in the courts of heaven.

Father, right now, in the name of Jesus, I now ask You to command, in the name of Jesus and by the power of Jesus' blood, that every fallen angel, demon, infirmity and familiar spirit leave me by coming out of my soul and body and every part of me, all the generations walking the earth and all future generations, our DNA, chemical body make up and our blood lines.

I now thank and praise the Father of all creation for my salvation, healing, deliverance, and freedom from curses and poverty in Christ Jesus. I thank you Father for restoring me to my full inheritance in Christ Jesus and my the nations praise Your glorious name forever and ever, Amen.

REFERENCES

Amplified Bible (AMP)

Copyright © 2015 by The Lockman Foundation, La Habra, CA 90631

The Holy Bible, New King James Version

Copyright © 1982 by Thomas Nelson, Inc. Nelson, Thomas. Holy Bible, New King James Version (NKJV) . Thomas Nelson. Kindle Edition.

New American Standard Bible-NASB 1995 (Includes Translators' Notes)

Copyright © 1960, 1962, 1963, 1968, 1971, 1972, 1973, 1975, 1977, 1995 by The Lockman Foundation

A Corporation Not for Profit, La Habra, California

All Rights Reserved

The Lockman Foundation. New American Standard Bible-NASB 1995 (Includes Translators' Notes) (Kindle Locations 1410-1412). The Lockman Foundation. Kindle Edition.

Logos Bible Software 7 - Copyright 1992-2018 Faithlife/Logos Bible Software.

© 1998 by InterVarsity Christian Fellowship/ USA ® All rights reserved. No part of this publication may be reproduced, stored in a retrieval system or transmitted in any form or by any means, electronic, mechanical, photocopying, recording or otherwise, without the prior permission of InterVarsity Press.

Leland Ryken, James C. Wilhoit, Tremper Longman III. Dictionary of Biblical Imagery (p. 1058). InterVarsity Press. Kindle Edition.

Derek Prince MP3 - The Old Self And New Self

NOTES

EXPLORING SECRETS
OF THE
HEAVENLY REALMS

VOL. 1

AVAILABLE ON NOW AMAZON

Exploring Secrets of the Heavenly Realms

Vol. 3

Coming Soon
Available on Amazon

Made in the
USA
Lexington, KY